A Socio-Economic Study of

Company Paintings

Contours of Indian Art & Architecture

1. The Panorama of Jaipur Paintings; by Rita Pratap; (ISBN 978-81-246-0068-9)
2. Islamic Tombs in India — The Iconography and Genesis of Their Design; by Fredrick W. Bunce (ISBN 978-81-246-0245-4)
3. Feminine Beauty in Indian Art and Literature; by T.N. Mishra (ISBN 978-81-246-0387-1)
4. A Socio-Economic Study of Company Paintings (CE 1757-1857); by T.N. Mishra (ISBN 978-81-246-0571-4)

Contours of Indian Art & Architecture, no. 4

A Socio-Economic Study of Company Paintings

(CE 1757-1857)

T.N. Mishra

D.K. Printworld (P) Ltd.
Publishers of Indian Traditions

Cataloging in Publication Data — DK
[Courtesy: D.K. Agencies (P) Ltd. <docinfo@dkagencies.com>]

Mishra, T. N. (Tej Narain), 1945-
A socio-economic study of company paintings, CE 1757-1857 / T.N. Mishra.
p. cm. — (Contours of Indian art & architecture ; no. 4.)
Includes bibliographical references (p.).
ISBN 13: 9788124605714
ISBN 10: 8124605718

1. Company painting – Social aspects. 2. Company painting – Economic aspects. 3. India – In art. I. Title. II. Series: Contours of Indian art & architecture ; no. 4.

DDC 759.954 22

ISBN 13: 978-81-246-0571-4 ISBN 10: 81-246-0571-8
First published in India, 2011

Published and printed by:
D.K. Printworld (P) Ltd.
Regd. Office: 'Srikunj', F-52, Bali Nagar
Ramesh Nagar Metro Station
New Delhi – 110 015-13
Phones: (011) 2545 3975; 2546 6019 *Fax*: (011) 2546 5926
E-mail: indology@dkprintworld.com
Website: www.dkprintworld.com

Preface

ART reflects contemporary society. This holds good also with reference to Company Paintings. Like other source materials, the art of the period possesses tremendous potentialities in reconstructing the social history of the Company Period. A careful analysis of the Company paintings done on paper, glass, ivory, mica, etc. offers a graphic description on contemporary society.

For the study of social and economical life in the eighteenth and nineteenth centuries, our dependable source has been the painting of the periods. One of the principal criteria for the identification of this class of painting is the degree to which it observed the Indian scene in all its aspects, including history and society. The company painting in its heyday, during eighteenth century carefully observed and recorded the life as such.

Art reflects contemporary society. This maxim holds good also for that group of paintings which was designated in the late eighteenth century as Company Paintings. Pictures painted on cheap paper (*firkās*) or machine-made Western paper, laid bare a life lived in palaces, waysides, villages and small towns. These depicted the princes and people, beggars and saints, traders and merchants, animals and birds, religious and secular architecture, means of transport, different castes and creeds, and people engaged in different professions — in fact, it revealed the graphic picture of the contemporary period.

The term "Company Paintings" has been coined by Indian art historians to denote a special group of paintings, which was evolved due to an interaction between traditional Indian paintings and European paintings of eighteenth and nineteenth centuries CE. This class of painting thus evolved and illustrated Indian socio-political life, birds, animals, personal portraits, etc. This new style of painting included European perspectives, light and shade, colour combination, and utilization of machine-made paper, etc. Certain scholars preferred to designate this new idiom as "Patna Painting" while others called it "Firaṅgī-Kalā." The name "Company School" appears to be the most appropriate one, since this style evolved during the tenure of the East India Company's rule in India and most of the scholars in the field approved of this name. This art style developed through European contact and had spread in most of the art centres of India; each centre maintained certain distinctive features of its own and is identifiable by distinct regional flavour and provincial character too.

Before the advent of the so-called Company style, the whole of northern India witnessed a group of paintings entitled Later Mughal School in which one finds the decadence of Imperial Mughal School flavour, skill and competence. Mughal miniatures show certain things that were never seen before in India, and their lasting effects reverberated throughout India even after the Mughals. The Mughal emperors were keen lovers of nature and art, and their personalities were, to a certain extent, reflected in art and culture of their time.

The Mughals were in contact with European traders and missionaries from the period of Akbar and, therefore, mention requires to be made here that the impact of European paintings was deeply felt in the development of the Mughal painting. By virtue of the novelty and fineness or fine technical quality of the Western art, the Mughal artists realized their own shortcomings, and introduced considerable improvement in the technique of shadowing, modelling and perspective and the inspirations came from the West. The traits which they accepted from the West were thoroughly integrated in their style in such a way that nothing remains visible other than some faint traces of technical details.

Mughal painting lost much of its glamour and refinement within a few years after Jahangir's death. Though Shahjahan was interested in miniatures and illustrated manuscripts in his days, his enthusiasm was kept reserved for architecture. On the other hand, Aurangzeb who succeeded him was so orthodox and averse to painting that the highly developed art of miniature painting headed for steady decline. The court artists began to feel insecure in the absence of support, encouragement and patronization and were even compelled to leave Delhi in search of means of sustenance elsewhere. The painters thus chose to migrate to the court of other favourable patrons. The centres for artists were thus shifted to other regions. Consequently, one finds the evolution of so-called Later Mughal School of Painting. This new idiom was also called paintings of the provincial Mughals. The provincial Mughal Schools were characterized by different traditions but they did not change their basic traits and style within their own framework. Such provincial styles in art forms were born, developed and were recognized as new style because of the encouragement and patronage that was lost in due course of time. In forthcoming years mutual conflict, attack and counter-attack by kings and *nawāb*s, external intrusions, the "divide and rule" policy adopted by the Britishers and their political interferences, shattered central and provincial powers. The prevailing turbulence and indomitable environment caused fear, panic and insecurity among artists — now they neither had any encouragement nor any support. They wandered here and there in search of livelihood, and again started the misfortune of artists and the situations threatened the stand of Indian traditional painting too.

Advent of the seventeenth century saw European traders, viz. the Portuguese, the Dutch, the French and British, and these traders started combining amongst themselves for establishing authority in India. Ultimately, the British East India Company, also called as "John Company" was finally successful in establishing both trade as well as their "colony." The British East India Company set up various business establishments all over India and also built forts and garrisons to protect themselves.

With the influx of traders and the British army there came a number of painters to seek their fortunes in India and brought along with them new techniques and styles. And this was the time when the Indian artists started incorporating certain European techniques in their works in order to gain confidence among their new possible buyers. Today what's known as the Company School of Art was thus finally evolved. Not only Europeans resided in India but also people of divergent professions and disciplines settled here who were proficient in their works. Some of them were artists and were experts in Western style. Of these, mention may be made of Sir Charles D'Oyly, Emily Eden, Daniels, Tilly Kettle, Capt. Robert Smith, James Prinsep, Markham Kitto, William Hodge, etc. They travelled all over India, saw the people, the society and their cultural activities and sketched them with their brushes. They brought new techniques and bequeathed them to the local artists. Hereafter, the Indian artists started sketching and painting with imported materials and began to paint not on a prepared ground (*wasli*) but on machine-made paper and learnt to draw in pencil or in sepia wash direct on to the paper. They modified their colour scheme; flat patterns with bright patches of colour were replaced by soft rounded form, light and shade being indicated by soft washes of colour. Different frames were used to introduce perspective of the Western type.

With certain marked exceptions, Company Painting took much the same form in every centre. The favourite subjects were costumes, castes, crafts, trades, methods of transport and conveyances, washermen, butlers returning from the market, tailors, maid-servants and sweepers exercising the dogs. They portray the various bazaar tradesmen and craftsmen, peddlers, bangle-sellers, fish-sellers, butchers, basket-makers, sweetmeat-sellers, water-carriers, brass-workers, blacksmiths; they painted familiar town and village sights, school master with pupils, women grinding *dal* or spinning or going to temple to worship, scenes of Indian social activities such as wedding, music and dancing parties, nautch girls, gambling men, milkmen and women, palanquins, pilgrims, etc. In these sets, each trade, craft or occupation was shown with identifying attributes — a bricklayer with measure and trowel, shoe-maker with awl and shoe, a cook with chicken and kettle, method for pressing oil and sugar and in this way we get a convenient pictorial guide to social and economic life of society. Town and village occupations with their unfamiliar materials and tools also aroused interest and were recorded.

Earlier, in the previous century, the Indians and Europeans met each other in easy equality and had been mutually interested in each other's ways of life but the rise of East India Company changed that relationship to that of a ruling race and a subject people. The web of diplomatic and commercial relations in which East India Company found itself involved now that had become a "country power" took its agents to courts all over India. Representatives of the company appeared at the court of Delhi, where the Great Mughal still maintained the pretence of imperial majesty and exercised a nominal suzerainty of India; including those of the company itself found in one scene of such painting. A few depictions show that European settlements in India lived their own life, with their own shape, newspapers, concerts and entertainments. They lived their own world isolated from all individual feeling or sympathy. The result is an utter absence of those ties between the governors and the governed. This observation of India by professional artists was extended by the work of amateur artists. The graceful dress of Indian women was appreciated but the constraints of *purdāh* made it almost impossible for artists to depict women of good family or rank and they were limited to drawing village women, dancing girls or the Indian mistresses of the British officials.

The Company Paintings are now seen as an important part of Indian history since they provided a record of social and economical life of India and Indian people — specially the soldiers in the service of Indian princes, armed with half-pikes, sabres, matchlocks and shields, companies of merchants, palanquin-bearers making *chapatti*s, bands of religious devotees engaged in worship, travelling *fakīr*s, families with their women in hackeries and men escorting them on little horses and bullocks, it was not uncommon to see the manufacturer at his loom in the cool shade, attended by his friend softening his labour by the tender strain of music. Such subjects arranged in sets, provided conspectus of social life in India. One further type of social documents must be noted. As the British extended their power, they came into contact with Indian rulers, emperor, *nawābs* and with a local *rājā*. Artists were at time deputed or commissioned to commemorate *durbar*, levees, banquets and entertainments and in this way a new subject entered in Company Painting.

An analysis would show that whether a man is a trader or a participant in a festival, each one is seen depicted with hollow, anxious eyes with their straining figure racked by poverty. Domestic servants were normally presented with quiet dignity and unobtrusive grace. Their smooth postures and flowing robes suggested the calm assurance of British establishments. This concentration of servants normally involved certain types; each servant was depicted with individuality. In certain instances company painters transcended the general survey of clerks, housemaids, tent-pitchers, cultivators, maid playing with children, typical servants painted with ceremonious poise; particular servants are shown at time with almost noble gravity, the painters contriving to interpret their manner. The whole status of servants in company households or British establishments is thus depicted.

The concentration on trades and occupation normally involved certain types. Each mode was depicted with peculiarity — a large inland trade was maintained effectively by organised caravan and river-borne traffic, a network of banking and wholesale mercantile establishment in all the trade and industrial centres of India with branches and the system of the payment, caravans and *kāfilās* travelled long distances. The trade in foodgrains was in the hand of *baṅjārās* who move from one part of the country to another in the bullock convoys. These are also found included in painting sets which show the situation of eighteenth century.

In the eighteenth century the artisan class did not live in prosperity even in those areas where the fabricated luxury goods were in constant demand in the provincial and imperial courts. The interference of the administration went to the extent of monopolising looms to secure special trading privileges for officials, or a ban was imposed on the use, purchase and sale of certain items. Therefore, prices of articles depended not only on the annual rainfall but also on monopolistic conditions and cost of carriage. For foodgrains there could be only local markets. The European merchants employed their own salaried servants, who exploited the artisans even more.

Painted in oil or in water colour or drawn in sepia or pencil, the paintings of this period revealed a pathetic Indian scenario. The painful countenances, faces without smile, blank looks, figures pervaded with nervous tensions are enough evidences to prove visually the economically deprived people, shaky, panicky, unstable and unaware of their future. The paintings depict the saga of a struggle for subsistence and survival.

Acknowledgement

IN the collections of related materials for this volume the author is indebted to many scholars and institutions. Of these, mention may be made of those scholars who have been consulted during the preparation of this volume; their contributions are mentioned in the bibliography.

I am grateful for the help and suggestions of Prof. Dr Deena Bandhu Pandey, formerly Head, Department of History of Art, Banaras Hindu University and Prof. Tapati Lahiri, Department of English, A.M. Post Graduate College, Varanasi who have gone through the manuscript and made valuable suggestions.

My thanks are due to Bharat Kala Bhavan, especially to the sections of painting and photography for help and co-operation. I am equally thankful to the National Museum, New Delhi, and the State Museum, Lucknow, Bharat Kala Bhawan Library, Library at the Department of Ancient Indian History, Culture and Archaeology, and the Central Library of Banaras Hindu University.

I am thankful to my wife and my daughters, who gave me encouragement in preparation of the manuscript.

Thanks are also due to Sanskriti: Shodh evam Prakashan, Varanasi, for preparation of the script.

T.N. Mishra

Contents

1

Evolution of the Company School of Art

EAST India Company[1] was established in England around sixteenth century. During Jahangir's reign an English officer, Captain Middleton was granted permission for residing and doing business in the city of Surat, in the year 1611.[2] After having a stronghold over the city, he further extended his business establishment towards the western coast of India, as in the Bay of Khambat, Bombay, Ahmedabad and Bharuch,[3] then around the year 1613 Golakuṇḍā's administrator authorised the English traders to carry on business throughout his state — thus slowly and steadily they constructed their business centres there. In 1639 these English traders built-up a fort at Madras and named it "Fort Saint George."

Gradually the English traders marched northwards to extend their sway in Orissa. They established another centre at Balasore, situated on the border of Bengal and Orissa and one at Hariharpur on the Mahānadī Delta. In 1651 another British establishment came into being at Hooghly. In due course of time, the Britishers disseminated to different parts of the country to places like Patna, Kasim Bazaar and Rājmahal. Simultaneously, they also established a trade centre at Sutanuti which was later strongly fortified. This place subsequently came to be known as Calcutta.

The Britishers came to India with the aim of trade and business. But the political unrest and mismanagement inspired them to change their trade policy. And the so-called "John Company" then decided to strengthen all their business centres. The Britishers gave up their previous policy of political non-interference and limiting themselves to trade only and started visualizing their ambitions of establishing a British Empire in India, for which the prevailing political conditions and unrest paved the way. Disintegration of the Mughal Empire, revolts and crisis among various sections of society, increasing rivalry and mutual confrontations among Indian kings and *nawābs*, deteriorating central authority of the provincial governments and above all sporadic external attacks prepared the hotbed of Indian polity and helped the East India Company cash in on the situation to give shape to their empirical policy.[4] English governors strengthened the foundation of English rule in India with their mischievous policies. The policy was given a start by Lord Clive, Warren Hastings, Lord Wellesley and Sir John Shore and was completed with the promulgation of the Doctrine of Lapse by Lord Dalhousie.[5] After the "First Freedom War of 1857" the British rule was straightaway imposed upon India, replacing Company rule, and India then on became a British colony.

At the time of English intrusion Mughal art including Mughal painting in general was at its apex. Mughal painting evolved during Akbar's regime and was cultivated with sustained interest. This art developed mainly with a combination of Indian and Iranian elements. The great Akbar fostered a forceful art and architectural style with assimilation of the various art traditions and ideals, indigenous as well as foreign. He laid the foundation of the Mughal School of Painting and Mughal School of Architecture. Indeed Akbar took an important part in the evolution of Mughal culture by the happy fusion and harmonious blending of Persian and Indian cultures; he himself was the very symbol of that synthesis. He gave a new orientation to Indo-Islamic history. Jahangir ascended the throne on 3 November 1605. Under his enlightened patronage, there was an all round progress in every walk of life, but his first virtue lies in artistic development. He was a keen lover of nature and art and his personality was, to a certain extent, reflected in the art and culture of his time. His reign, on the whole, was fruitful of peace and prosperity to the Empire. Under his auspices industry and commerce progressed, architecture achieved notable triumphs, painting reached its high water marks, and literature flourished as it had never done before. Jahangir's India strove hard to create new convention by freely borrowing the techniques, decorative details and artistic themes from other countries.

At the beginning of Shahjahan reign, there was little change in the course of miniature painting; artists stayed on in the imperial employ and continued to paint in the same styles. Shahjahan's interests in painting were never as involved as those of his father, however, nor is there any indication that he participated in creating them as did Jahangir. The protocol that dominated the court functions is easily discernible in imperial painting. Works generally became more linear as well as more meticulous, and it is possible to compare the coolness of his picture with the pristine white marble he used for construction or gems he prized. He seems to have viewed painting purely as a decorative art and therefore, did not require the same expressiveness from his miniaturists as did Jahangir. But he encouraged this art and got duplicated some of the finest European paintings.

An English ambassador Sir Thomas Roe wrote in his traveller's diary that he presented the emperor with a painting with the thought that nobody in India would be able to make a copy of the painting. But he was astounded on being presented with six copies of the same piece and it took him some time to recognise the original painting.[6] Once he (Thomas Roe) presented a watch to prince Shahjahan; on receiving it, the prince remarked that an oil painting would have been a better gift.[7] The context of the above references reveal that the Europeans began to establish a friendly relation with the court at the time of Akbar and this attitude received momentum during Jahangir's regime. The Europeans brought paintings with them to the court which were copied subsequently by Indian painters by the order of the emperor.

The Mughals were in contact with European traders and missionaries from the period of Akbar, and therefore, mention requires to be made here about the import of European art on the development of Mughal painting. By virtue of the novelty, fineness or fine technical quality of Western art, the Mughal artists realised their own shortcomings, and introduced considerable improvement in their technique of shadowing and modelling perspective, and the inspiration came from the West. The traits which they accepted from the West were thoroughly integrated in their style, in such a way that nothing tangibly European was noticed.[8] There is no hesitation to accept the European impact that was steadily coming upon Indian painters. Dara Shikoh's portrait, which was sketched in an ovoid frame, is totally based upon European technique. This style was subsequently adopted by artists like Balchand, Mohammed Hashim and Chittarman who were in his court.[9]

The above reference is given in the context of expressing that European art was being copied since Akbar's regime and its effect started appearing explicitly in Indian painting from Jahangir's period, and such impact is found usually in the treatment of the background and light-shade of the paintings. But, by then Indian painting had become strong enough in itself to intermingle and absorb these European effects.

Shahjahan's third son, Aurangzeb, took the title of "Ālamgīr" (seizer of the universe), when he assumed the throne after imprisoning his father. Despite his religious purity and thoughtfulness on a personal level, his policies tore down what his great-grandfather Akbar had built. His policies were the most destructive to the empire. Before his death, Aurangzeb was aware of many of his grim follies. His reign from 1658 to 1707 was turbulent marked by political chaos and cultural stagnation in the Mughal court. Imperial patronage of art in the court of Delhi declined compelling artists to seek employment elsewhere, in local court in provinces. He was immersed in religion, in calligraphy and in the care of the state.

In spite of his later austerity, which turned him against music, dance and painting, a few of the best Mughal paintings were made for him. Perhaps, the painters realised that he might close the workshop and therefore, exuded themselves on his behalf. For whatever reason, this *durbar* is of stunning quality. The awesomely dignified emperor holds a hawk, while seated on an elegantly unpretentious gold throne beneath a canopy adorned with birds of paradise. In absence of tutelage and encouragement from the Delhi court, artists migrated towards provincial patrons. Mughal art, just like the Mughal Empire is marked by its rise, development, maturity, decadence and disintegration.[10] In its later phase it lost its vigour and excellence and was left as a mean copy of European art prices. On the other hand, weak administration and lack of patronage ultimately gave rise to the supremacy of the regional styles. These regional styles grew up with different local and regional characteristics.

Mughal painting lost much of its glamour and refinement within a few years after Jahangir's death. Though Shahjahan was interested in miniatures and illustrated manuscripts, later his enthusiasm became reserved for architecture. On the other hand, Aurangzeb who succeeded him was so orthodox and averse to painting that the highly developed art of miniature painting headed for steady decline. Court artists began to feel insecure in the absence of support, encouragement and patronization and were compelled to leave Delhi in search for means of subsistence elsewhere. The artists thus chose to migrate to the courts of other favourable patrons. The centres for artists' activities were shifted to other regions. Thus one finds the evolutions of later Mughal School of Painting. These new idioms were also called painting during the provincial Mughals. The provincial Mughals characterised by different traditions did not change basic traits and style within their own framework. In the seventeenth century Rājasthānī styles became famous for their local and regional character, in Rājpūtānā and its various centres. These were Mewaṛ, Būndī, Nāthdwārā, Amber, Jodhpur, Kishangarh, Bikaner, etc. where a blend of Rājasthānī–Mughal style evolved; these tendencies were also noticed to a certain extent in Bundelkhand. Painting of the hills of Basohli also evinced the impact of this Rājasthāṇī–Mughal style painting.[11]

Champa, Nurpur, Jasrota, Guler, Kangra, Mandi, Kullu, Nahan, etc. became the centres of hill paintings. The characteristic features of Basohli and Kangra Schools told largely upon the other hill schools mentioned already. Nearly all human sentiments, expressions and moods were depicted in the works of artists of the above two schools. The Garhwal School also bears traces of impact of the artistic idioms of Kangra. During the reign of King Sansar Chand (1774-1823) the Kangra School of Painting attained its classical acme. Not a single expression was left to be depicted by these artists. This is also evident in the Garhwal paintings.

In the seventeenth century, India became famous for its paintings. South India could not remain untouched by the migration of artists from the Mughal courts. All the paintings of this time exhibit certain Mughal mannerisms and elements.[12] South Indian paintings too show European effects, besides the Mughal ones[13] and came to be known as the "Deccan style." Bījāpur, Ahmednagar and Golakuṇḍā were the main centres of this style of art. Hyderabad, in due course, was recognized also as an art centre, and its style came to be designated as "Hyderabad style."

Such provincial styles in art form were born, developed and were recognised as new style because of the encouragement and patronage that was provided to them by regional kings and *nawābs*.[14] But this tendency was lost in due course of time. In forthcoming years mutual conflict, attack and counter-attack by kings and *nawābs*, external intrusions, the "divide and rule" policy adopted by the Britishers and their political interference, shattered central as well as provincial powers. The prevailing turbulent and indomitable environment caused fear, panic and insecurity among artists; now they neither had any encouragement nor any support. They wandered here and there in search of a livelihood and again restarted the misfortune of artists and Indian traditional painting too. Creative urge and artistic subtleties gradually diminished. The artists kept on trying to pursue their age-old techniques but failed to bring in the refines of the past. Standards deteriorated much; the art became commercial and cheap, and air of exhaustion, in every aspect, became more pronounced.

Artists looked for works in Murshidabad, Lucknow, Hyderabad, Patna and Benares.[15] Local administrators, who became independent because of deteriorating central autonomy encouraged them. Besides the local kings and administrators, the elite class of society and foreigners took an initial interest in these degenerating forms of art.

Advent of the seventeenth century saw European traders, viz. the Portuguese, the Dutch, the French and the British, competing amongst themselves for establishing authority in India. Ultimately the British East India Company, then also called as "John Company," was finally successful in establishing both trade as well as their vision of India. To give shape to their "colony," the British East India Company set up various business establishments all over India and also built forts and garrisons to protect themselves.

With the influx of traders and British army, came to India a number of painters to seek their fortunes and brought along with them new techniques and styles. And this was the time when the Indian artists started incorporating certain European techniques in their works in order to gain confidence among their new possible buyers. During the end of the eighteenth century, around 50 English artists are known to have come to India with the aim of earning money. Some of them were experts in their profession.[16] These artists made portraits of kings, *nawāb*s and rich connoisseurs to earn fortunes and their work was greatly adored. These portraits were in great demand which resulted in the end of the traditional style of "Bazaar painting."

Europeans could not keep themselves aloof from the local environment and way of life. They observed the ways of living, customs, festivals and wrote about these exotic experience to their friends and relatives back home. Some of them who knew sketching or painting represented India through their art and others commissioned local artists to make pictures for them to send abroad. Though such art pieces had no technical or artistic accuracy, yet they were in great demand for their exotic quality. A large number of sketches were sent on business level. But slowly the demand for such pieces decreased because these pictures had neither the charming quality of Indian art nor the attraction of the provincial style. These were mere shadows of the age-old paintings without any trace of refineness of the Mughal or provincial style. Therefore, these sketches could not maintain their attraction for a span of time, although they had unsuccessful attempts to adopt a few techniques of European art to improve themselves.[17] Not only Europeans resided in India but, people of divergent professions and disciplines settled here who were proficient in their work.[18] Some of them were artists who were experts in Western style. Of these, mention may be made of Charles D'Oyly, William Daniels, Thomas Daniels, Tilly Kettle, Capt. Robert Smith, James Prinsep, Markham Kitto, William Hodge, etc. They travelled all over India, saw the people, society and their cultural activities and sketched them with their brushes. They brought new techniques and bequeathed them to the local artists.[19] Hereafter the Indian artists started sketching and painting with imported materials and began to paint in watercolour on European machine-made paper.[20] They ceased to paint on a prepared ground (*wasli*) and learnt to draw in pencil or in sepia wash direct on to the paper. They modified their colour scheme; flat patterns with bright patches of colour were replaced with rounded form, light and shade being indicated with soft washes of colour. Different planes were also represented by perspective of the Western type.[21] And today what is known as the Company School of Art was, thus, finally evolved. But at the same time the Indian artists did not leave their age-old Indian style either. They blended the European style with the ethnic ones and this new style lasted for a long time.[22]

This new style, produced by the combination of European and Indian styles of painting, gave rise to a new school known as "Company School of Art."[23] Few scholars preferred to call it "Patna-painting" or "Patna style Painting" and other few named it as "Firaṅgī Kalā"[24] or Company School. This art style, evolved and developed through the European contact and spread to India, is identifiable by distinct regional and provincial characteristics too.[25] Company style painting spread in the country with the spread of Europeans, especially the Britishers. Local artists adopted the new style, leaving their "bazaar techniques" and made according to the Europeans' taste. The company style grew without any hurdle throughout eighteenth and nineteenth centuries.

When Europeans started dwelling in the southern states, the impact of this style was felt in these regions too. During the reign of Adil Shah II (1640) of Bījāpur "Deccan portraits" were made within ovoid framework, which was a characteristically European mannerism.[26] Individual portraits cast in oval framework was a common feature in Europe. An Italian writer Nicolas Manuchi needed some sketches to complete his book on Indian lifestyle, which was in four volumes. In the year 1702 he assigned local artists to prepare sketches under his directions. These sketches though based on Indian subjects were worked in European technique. They were made on plain backgrounds and both light and dark colours were used to show the effects of light and shade.[27]

Even when the company style was at its apex, the Mughal style of painting could not be entirely withdrawn from the Indian scene. Both the styles were in practice in certain centres of the country; for example in Benares, the families of Ustad Mool Chand and Ram Prasad were famous for their continued activities in Mughal style. The company style of painting was also produced by them as and when required. Mool Chand was famous for his ivory-painting and Ram Prasad made his own portrait in the "Company style" the example of which can still be seen in the collection of Bharat Kala Bhavan Museum in Varanasi. It can be said that the artists working in Mughal style, also respected the Company style and did not hesitate in adopting certain techniques of this European style, most often in the preparation of portraits in oval frames. Just like the artists working in Mughal style adopted features of the Company style in their works, those who basically worked in Company style did the vice versa. The most commonly adopted feature of the Company School artists was in the treatment of borders of painting. Many of their works can be seen with these Mughal style borders. An example of this bordered painting in feature by the Company School can be seen in Bharat Kala Bhavan, Varanasi as well as in other Indian museums. Beautiful golden lining works of Mughal School were executed with the help of European watercolours. Though the tendency of working in a mixed style, in art, is common, however, these paintings based upon Indo–European techniques failed miserably in producing quality paintings and appeared lifeless most of the times.

By the middle of the nineteenth century the entire administrative and political powers shifted into the hands of British government from those of John Company.[28] The entire country was now under the control of Britishers. Many British workers, officers and their family members visited India frequently. These comprised persons from different professions and every walk of life. They minutely observed every detail here, and started studying the activities of the populace and the luxurious lifestyle of the royalty. The medium of some of the artists to note their observations was through their brushes and colours.[29] With certain marked exception, company painting took much the same form in every centre. And this style was in vogue throughout the country but many paintings evinced at times certain differences, in accordance with the essence of different centres. These differences are traceable in local and provincial painting patterns. The result of this absorption of provincial and local patterns in Company style is distinct in south India's "Deccan style" and "Mughal style" prevalent in north India.

References

1. R.C. Mazumdar (ed.), *The Mughal Empire*, Bombay, 1974, p. 511.
2. Ibid.; A.L. Basham (ed.), *A Cultural History of India*, London, 1975, pp. 417, 471.
3. R.C. Mazumdar, op. cit., pp. 511, 512.
4. A.L. Basham (ed.), *A Cultural History of India*, p. 56.
5. For detailed study, see R.C. Mazumdar (ed.), *British Paramountcy and Indian Renaissance*, Part I, Bombay, 1970; T.N. Mishra, *Banārasa meṅ Kampanī Śailī kī Citrakalā* (in Hindi), Varanasi, 1992.
6. Rai Krishna Das, *Bhārata ki Citrakalā* (Hindi), Allahabad, 1974, p. 90; T.N. Mishra, *Westernisation of Indian Art*, New Delhi, 1996, p. 25.
7. Ibid.
8. Ibid.
9. M.C. Beach, *The Grand Mughal Imperial Painting in India 1600-60*, U.S.A., 1978, pp. 100 & 167; F.M. Archer, *Indian Miniature in the India Office Library*, London, 1981, p. 401; T.N. Mishra, op. cit., p. 26.
10. T.N. Mishra, *Westernisation of Indian Art*, 1996, p. 26.
11. Ibid., p. 27.
12. Moti Chandra, "Dakani Kalam; Bijapur", *Kalā Nidhi* (in Hindi), varṣa 1, aṅka 1, pp. 34, 41.
13. Ibid., p. 39; Mildred Archer, *Indian Miniature in the India Office Library*, 1981, p. 502.
14. A.L. Basham (ed.), *A Cultural History of India*, pp. 330-31; R.C. Mazumdar, *The Mughal Empire*, p. 819.
15. Moti Chandra, *Technique of Mughal Painting*,

Lucknow, 1949, pp. 98-99.

16. T.N. Mishra, *Banārasa meṅ Kampanī Śailī kī Citrakalā*, 1992, p. 12.
17. T.N. Mishra, 1996, op. cit., p. 29.
18. Mildred Archer, *Patna Painting*, London, 1947, p. 688.
19. Ibid., p. 11.
20. Mildred Archer, op. cit., p. 27; P.C. Manuk, "The Patna School of Painting", *Journal of the Bihar Research Society*, vol. XXIX, 1943, p. 161; T.N. Mishra, 1992, op. cit., p. 14.
21. T.N. Mishra, 1996, op. cit., p. 30.
22. Loc. cit.
23. Mulk Raj Anand, *Album of Indian Painting*, Delhi, 1973, p. 160; W.G. Archer, *Bazaar Paintings of Calcutta*, London, 1953; Rai Krishna Das, *Bhārata kī Citrakalā* (in Hindi), Allahabad, 1974, p. 110; F. M. Archer, op. cit., p. 130; T.N. Mishra, 1996, op. cit., p. 30.
24. R.C. Manuk, *The Patna School of Paintings*, p. 147; Mildred Archer, op. cit., preface (p. vii).
25. Mildred Archer, *Indian Popular Painting*, London, 1977, p. 144; T.N. Mishra, *Banārasa meṅ Kampanī Śailī kī Citrakalā* (in Hindi), p. 14.
26. F.M. Archer, op. cit., p. 502.
27. Mildred Archer, op. cit., p. 50.
28. A.L. Basham, op. cit., p. 4.
29. T.N. Mishra, 1992, op. cit., p. 16.

2

Techniques of Company Painting

A CAREFUL analysis of the company painting in the collections of different Indian and foreign museums reveals that the so-called painting of the "Company rule" blended certain foreign techniques into their traditional style of paintings. These techniques being mostly European, the paintings thus made using this blend of traditional Indian styles and European techniques came to be termed as the Indo–European style of painting. Gradually, the incorporation of European techniques became more and more pronounced and the paintings lost their Indian touch. A notable difference in these new trends is the use of pencil sketching.[1] The painter of this style first worked out the sketch of desired things and then they applied colours.[2] Whereas in the traditional Indian style the artists painted their themes directly with brushes, in the company style of painting, particularly in figure drawings, the artist sketched the faces first there are instances of company painting where the faces have been minutely sketched and painted but the rest of the figure left unfinished or finished summarily without much detail. In certain cases the traditional painters, instead of using pencils, used ash of charred tamarind or pigeon pea for painting.[3]

The Company artists used imported paper for their paintings.[4] The imported paper is of a very fine quality having smooth surfaces. The traditional Indian painters on the other hand used prepared board (*wasli*) for working out their paintings. The use of such board was less favoured by Company School artists. Through the watermarks on the paper of the company paintings, one can easily detect the place name where it had been manufactured. It is interesting to note that in some of the papers, the date of manufacture had also been indicated through watermarks. This has also helped in calculating the date of painting to some extent.[5] The use of board (*wasli*) for painting, though less favoured by the Company paintings, is not altogether unknown. These boards were made by pasting two or three papers and therefore they became thicker. A few company paintings have been traced, painted on such boards.[6]

The Company painters appear to have favoured imported watercolours for paintings. By and large, the Company painters made less use of traditionally prepared vegetable and mineral colours. The reason for this was quite obvious, as the preparation of the vegetable and mineral colours demanded lot of time and labour. Even during the later Mughal period the painters started using imported watercolours.[7] Therefore, the two basic requirements of paintings, viz. paper and colour, were imported from Europe during the Company Period.

Generally, the colours used by the Company painters were light and transparent. The watercolours were prepared using sufficient amount of gum. In general, gum Arabic (*babūla kā gonda*) was used as a popular adhesive. Colours used in such paintings were red, white, orange, vermilion, blue, yellow, green and black.[8] Besides this the use of gold and silver dust was also noticed.[9] Comparatively the use of silver has been lesser known during this period. In order to give a thick dripping effect, certain thick colours were used by the Company painters. The use of light white colour to make the outline clear and understandable had also been noticed in certain paintings.

Company painters used red and black ink, it is known as *lāla-kalaṁ* and "*śyāh-kalam*. In such style of painting, the brush was directly used and therefore, required the skill of an expert artist.[10] To the Europeans, this was known as "pen-ink" technique. Expressive and beautiful sketches were made in pencil by the European artists. In most cases these included portraits drawn with individual characteristics and liveliness. Some sketches done on postcards have also been detected. These small sketches were known to Indian artists during the later Mughal period too. These sketches on cheap paper are called *firkā* in which both religious and secular themes were depicted.[11] The Europeans introduced the important graphic art in India, which not only helped in enlarging or decreasing the size of painting but also helped in the preparation of copies of many popular common themes.

Ivory was another medium used for working out painting by the Company artists. The painting on ivory required much care and expertise. On ivory painting, light and transparent colours were used. The painters preferred working on new ivory sheets. In selecting ivory pieces, lot of care was taken — transparent, translucent or cracked ivory sheets were avoided for working out paintings. In few cases, stippling technique is found to have been adopted. The painters, after applying the first coat on ivory, waited for some time to let that coat dry and then applied the second coat on it. Beautiful examples of ivory paintings are found in various museums all over India.

Company painters were equally expert in mica painting. Paintings on mica reveal mature workmanship. Generally, watercolours were used for the painting on mica sheets. But the colours for mica painting were made thicker by adding adhesives. Occasionally, the uses of thin and transparent colours on mica have been detected but in such cases the artist's expertise was called for. Glass as a medium of painting has also been noticed during the Company Period. For painting on glass, oil colours were used and there are instances of finishing and re-touching by oil colours in the compositions on glass.[12] The traditional Indian painters had never used oil paints, therefore oil painting is considered to be a contribution of West in India. The tradition of painting portraits within an ovoid frame was noticed from the period of imperial Mughals,[13] but this was not an Indian technique and definitely came from Europe. A few portraits of Muslim administrators of Bījāpur (south India) and portraits of members of the royal families of Benares are also found incorporated within such ovoid frames.[14] The Company painters achieved great efficiency and fineness with regard to techniques of the Western world.

The tradition of giving ornamental or decorative borders (*hāśiyā*) to the painting, though lesser known during the Company Period, it was not altogether unheard of.[15] A number of sketches were made with single or double borders. In most cases where figure is outlined by ornamentation the borders included flowers, leaves, and creepers. In a number of Company paintings, the artists incorporated certain old traditions, like having Arabic, Persian and Urdu inscriptions on the paintings. But in most cases it is visually evident that the painter and scribe were two different persons. There are instances seen in Company paintings where the inscriptions are upside down. Had the painter and inscriber been the same, such a mistake would not have occurred. The inscriber in such cases seems not to have understood the right side of the composition.[16]

Generally, it had been found that the Indian artist while drawing a figure drew the face first and coloured it, but later did not finish the other parts of the figure. In certain cases, the artist is seen to have painted the body leaving the face untouched. Such instances are, however, very rare. A good artist sketched the human figure in pencil first, in an attempt to expose the physical characteristics of the person, then they wrote the names of the different colours to be used on different parts of the body, and then finally coloured them.[17] Occasionally, they took help of colour washes to bring out the effects of light and shade. The Company painters also exploited the European technique in order to bring out depth in their paintings.

It is very difficult to say anything about the brushes used by Company painters. Traditional artists made brushes using animal hairs but it appears that the Company painters used imported brushes and paper for their paintings, but the original tradition of making brushes from cat's, camel's or goat's hair and also from hair of a squirrel's tail continued. The traditional process of manufacturing brushes was termed as *kalam bāndhnā* and the person who made these brushes was called *"kalam kartāra."*

References

1. T.N. Mishra, *Banārasa meṅ Kampanī Śailī kī Citrakalā* (in Hindi), 1992, p. 35.
2. Mildred Archer, *Patna Painting*, p. 18; Moti Chandra, *The Techniques of Mughal Painting*, p. 38.
3. Moti Chandra, op. cit., pp. 35, 39.
4. Ibid., p. 99; T.N. Mishra, *Westernisation of Indian Art*, 1996, p. 38.
5. Moti Chandra, op. cit., p. 99; T.N. Mishra, op. cit., 1996, p. 31.
6. Moti Chandra, op. cit., pp. 35, 39.

7. T. N. Mishra, op. cit., 1996, p. 32.
8. Mildred Archer, *Company Drawing in the India Office Library*, p. 134.
9. Moti Chandra, op. cit., p. 99.
10. T.N. Mishra, *Westernisation of Indian Art*, p. 39.
11. Loc. cit.
12. P.C. Manuk, "The Patna School of Painting," *Journal of the Bihar Research Society*, 1943, vol. XXIX, p. 150; T.N. Mishra, 1992, op. cit., p. 40.
13. T.N. Mishra, op. cit., 1992, p. 23; T.N. Mishra, 1996, op. cit., p. 40.
14. Mildred Archer, op. cit., p. 12.
15. M.C. Beach, *Grand Mughal Imperial Painting in India* 1600-1660, U.S.A., pp. 100 and 167.
16. F.M. Archer, op. cit.; T.N. Mishra, 1996, op. cit., p. 41.
17. T.N. Mishra, 1992, op. cit., p. 37.

3

Centre and Theme of Company Painting

THERE were various centres where the Company painting developed with certain marked exceptions and took much the same form. Of these, a number of centres in south India appear to have come out as initial centres of this form of painting. Besides certain local features, most of the paintings of all these centres bear certain common features.[1] The Company paintings cover the period between eighteenth and twentieth centuries and these paintings laid bare the dramatic panorama of the lives of Indian people.

It was in south India that contact between Indians and Europeans first began to have a strong impact made by Indian artists for sale to Europeans. In Tanjore it was artists of the *mocī* caste (shoe-maker) who responded to this demand. The regions in the south also included Madras, Trichinopally, Puddukkottai, Malabar, Coorg and Hyderabad. Subsequently other centres came up. Of these, mention may be made of Cuttack, Calcutta, Murshidabad, Patna, Chhapra, Benares, Faizabad, Lucknow, Agra, Mathura, Delhi, Amritsar, Lahore and Kashmir. A few places in western India too became centres of Company Painting; mention may be made of Poona, Satara, Bombay, Belgaum, etc.

The Company paintings cover the period between eighteenth and twentieth centuries. The favourite subjects were costumes, castes, crafts, trade, method of transport and conveyances, washermen, butlers returning from market, maidservants exercising the dogs. The paintings portray the various bazaar, tradesman and craftsman, peddler, bangle-sellers, fish-sellers, butchers, basket-makers, sweetmeat-sellers, toddy-sellers, carpenters, distillers, thread-makers, blacksmith, goldsmith, candle-makers, water-carriers, brass-workers, polishers, barbers, messengers, roaming mendicants, musicians, birds, animals, flowers, plants, trees and fruits; they also included portraits of kings, *nawābs*, their subjects, courtiers, nobles and warriors. They painted familiar town and village sights, school master with pupils, women grinding *dal* or spinning or going to temple to worship, scenes of Indian social activities such as wedding, music and dancing parties, nautch-girls, gambling men, milkmen and women, palanquins, pilgrims, etc. In these sets, each trade, craft or occupation was shown with identifying attributes — a bricklayer with measure and trowel, shoe-maker with awl and shoe, a cook with chicken and kettle, method for pressing oil and sugar and in this way we get a convenient pictorial guide to the social and economic life of the society. Town and village occupations with their unfamiliar materials and tools also aroused interest and were recorded. Such paintings help us in reconstructing the socio-religious, political and ethnic history of the contemporary period. Along with the Company painters, the contemporary British painters also tried, in their own ways, to document their experiences of life in India. The subject matter of such artists included the day-to-day happenings around them and many exciting occurrences which appeared too fascinating to record. Certain social evils were also depicted through paintings of this period. It appears from these paintings that the artists must have been a witness to such evil instances.

A close analysis of these drawings, sketches and paintings of the persons engaged in various professions, like wealthy courtiers and their servants, employees of European officers or businessmen bears an expression of cold, pathetic gloom and exhibits an air of helplessness on their facial features. In a number of instances, it appears that the very life sap has been squeezed out of them. Same is the case with paintings of common people. It is noteworthy that trades-people in the bazaar, members of a procession or participants in a festival were often depicted with hollow, anxious eyes, their straining figures racked by poverty. It is not a mere record of private life; it is a study of manners, habits or customs. An air of unhappiness and frustration covers their expressions as painted by the Company artist. The socio-economic conditions prevalent during that time can be very easily ascertained by carefully studying the paintings of the Company Period. It must always be that until the invention of photography the completion of visual records of all kinds had to be made through the medium of drawing and painting, and such art had a genuinely scientific purpose.

Earlier, in the previous century, the Indians and Europeans had met with easy equality and had been mutually interested in each other's ways, but the rise of East India Company changed that relationship to that of a ruling race and a subject people. The web of diplomatic and commercial relations in which East India Company found itself involved now that it had become a "country power" took its agents to courts all over India. Representatives of the Company appeared at the court of Delhi, where the Great Mughal still maintained the pretence of imperial majesty and exercised a nominal suzerainty of India; including those of the Company itself had been found in one scene of such painting. A few depictions show that European settlements in India lived their own life, with their own shape, newspapers, concerts and entertainments. They lived their own world and isolated from all individual feeling or sympathy. The result is an utter absence of those ties between the governors and the governed. This observation of India by professional artists was extended by the work of amateur artists. The graceful dress of Indian women was appreciated but the constraints of *purdāh* made it almost impossible for artists to depict women of good family or rank and they were limited to drawing village women, dancing girls or the Indian mistress of the European officials.

The Company paintings are now seen as an important part of Indian history since they provided record of social and economic life of India and Indian people specially the soldiers in service of Indian princes, armed with half-pikes, palanquin-bearers, sabres, matchlocks and shields, companies of merchants, palanquin-bearers making *chapatti*s, bands of religious devotees engaged in worship, travelling *fakīr*s, families with their women in hackeries and men escorting them on little horses and bullocks; it was not uncommon to see the manufacturer at his loom in the cool shade, attended by his friend softening his labour by the tender strain of music. Such subjects, arranged in sets, provided concepts of social life in India.[2]

References

1. Mildred Archer, *Company Drawing in the India Office Library*, p. 7; T.N. Mishra, *Banārasa meṅ Kampanī Śailī kī Citrakalā* (in Hindi), 1992, p. 16.
2. Mildred Archer, *Patna Painting*, London, 1974, pp. 7-8.

4

Artistes and Their Social Status

THE character of the art of a country is very often determined by its physical conditions. The human mind cannot ignore external surroundings; and art is an expression of human thought and feeling. It invariably relates, consciously or unconsciously, to the physical conditions under which it finds expression. Thus we find that the variations and changes in the art of a country correspond to the vicissitudes through which it has to pass, and art is no exception. Indian art has a long history and shows a variety of artistic expressions of different periods. They help to understand the mental state of the Indian people under different conditions, their character and emotions; all of which contribute towards the varied artistic forms of the country.

The impact of European countries on India has brought about certain changes in many directions. Our consideration is painting here. We find that the elements of European country have effected the indigenous artistic expression of our country. In order to understand what this influence has been and how it has been brought about, one has to study the conditions out of which they have grown into artistic abilities. Political conditions alone do not necessarily bring about changes in the aesthetic expression of the country. There must be some other thing to influence the mental activities of the people in order to effect aesthetic changes.

In the Indian economic organisation, the artisans are given a fixed remuneration. They are given plots of land in lieu of their work. They work at things in which they especially excel and its object is achieved by influences of the artisan's environment, which evokes and trains any special aptitudes for arts and crafts. The artisans thus have leisure, freedom, hope and happiness, and they cannot but express them in their handiwork. Their handiwork rises to the level of a conscious artistic activity, full of joy in the expression of happy and noble ideas and ideals. The artisans rise to become artists.

In the eighteenth century the artisans class did not live in prosperity even in those areas where the fabricated luxury goods were in constant demand in provincial and imperial courts. The interference of the administration went to some extent of monopolising special trading privileges for officials, or a ban was imposed on the use, purchase and sale of certain items. Therefore, the prices of articles depended not only on the annual rainfall but also on monopolistic conditions and the cost of carriage.

It was the excessive price of the raw materials as well as the burden of miscellaneous charges levied on the artisans and their products which drove them into the clutches of the middle-man and the financier. Thus weavers and painters of cloths were exploited by the three agencies engaged in the process of production and distribution of goods by cashier, brokers and merchants; and consequently, the artisans could not overcome the periodic crises of scarcity and famine which left them altogether destitute, as is abundantly testified by the Surat and Madras factors, with reference to the weaving communities. On the other hand, since the market of the principal handicrafts and artistic industries was chiefly confined to the limited class of ruler aristocracy, there was little scope of expansion for this class of crafts. The break-up of the Mughal Empire and the defeat of Muslim and Hindu powers and the reduction of the remaining Indian rulers to the position of British feudatories caused widespread misery and disorder. The craftsmen who depended upon the Imperial court lost their livelihood, and as such painting, architecture and other arts declined. About the standard of living of artisans the contemporary foreign travellers and merchants give a very dark picture. They say that they did not have better houses, clothes and enough food while working hard from morning to night.[1]

If the artists and manufacturers were properly encouraged, the useful and fine arts would have flourished, but these unhappy men are continually treated with harshness, and inadequately remunerated for their labour. The rich will have every article at a cheap rate. When a *mansabdāra* requires the service of an artisan, he sends for him, employing force, if necessary, to make the poor man to work hard and after the task is finished, the cold and unfeeling lord pays, not according to the value of the labour, but agreeably to his own standard of fair remuneration, the artisan having reason to congratulate himself if it has not been given in part payment. How then can it be expected that any spirit of emulation should animate the artist or manufacturer? Instead of contending for a superiority or reputation, his only anxiety is to finish his work and to earn the pittance that will supply him with a piece of bread. The artists, therefore, who arrive at any eminence in their art were those only who were in the service of the king or some powerful Omarah (*mansabdāra*), and who work exclusively for their patron. One can very well think what type of painting could be produced under such duress. And that is why there is no justification in holding that these crude paintings produced under duress and oppressive tactics were forming a style of its own. They were the same as popular style and that is why it should go under one heading by the Bazaar style.

The affluent craftsmen too sought to sell their articles through peddlers, walking salesmen, known as *pherīvālā*. Nearly one half of the price of the articles was paid by them initially and the rest of the amount after the sale or within specified times. The peddlers carried the pack load of articles subsisting on their back from one locality to another and sold them piecemeal to the desired consumer after striking a favourable bargain.

The artisan depended upon the merchants for the sale of his wares and was impelled to seek cash in advance for the purchase of raw material and the essential accessories. The luxuriant variety of articles were manufactured. Coarse cloth was woven almost in every village. Cotton-dyeing and printing was prevalent in several regions.

The premier cottage industries were cotton and silk textiles, manufacturing of iron, glass, arms, construction of boats, oils, perfumes, etc. and besides these cottage industries mentioned so far, there were various subsidiary industries to which the people engaged themselves in addition to their other manufacturing or agricultural pursuits. Bengal was a jute producing area, and hand-woven jute formed a subsidiary industry of local people. Bengal trade in gunny bag was in a flourishing condition till middle of the nineteenth century. Lac-rearing and manufacture, paper-making, soap-making, glass manufacture and stone-cutting, working in ivory and buffalo horn, making of gold ornaments, wooden furniture, pottery, carpentry, tanning and shoe-making formed some other subsidiary industries. These, like most other industries, were organised on domestic basis. Every weaver's house looked like a workshop and scarcely any village was without such weaving centres. The creative energies of the young vigorous people went into their work and forms and designs emerged which bear the imprint of this vigour and creativity. The craftsmen through their wares expressed the sensitivity and aspirations of the total community. And as such the artisans rose to become artists. The conditions of this type are true to a normal, healthy and vigorous national life, when the national genius and temper express themselves in ever-renewed types, forms and art-construction.

The cottage industry is not merely a form of livelihood; in this country it has been the main channel through which the creative impulses of its people have found expression. India has never had an art tradition separate from a craft tradition. It has only had a vigorous anonymous craft tradition. The great masterpieces of stone in the country is the evidence of skill and creative energies of the tradition of craftsmanship.

In the town, urban centres of production and distribution, separate localities for different craftsmen existed. The localities were known after the trades, viz. Khaṭiwāṛā, Chipaws, Mochiwāḍā, Koliwāḍā, Lohāran, Dhobiyāna, Malahiya-ṭolā, Machalī-bazaar, etc. Many streets were named after the community of craftsmen such as, Kharadiān, Mohallā Lohāran, Kamāigaran, Taliyāna, Kaṭarā Neel, etc. Hindus and Muslims were engaged amicably in different crafts and trades. Most of them were grouped in castes bearing the caption of specified vocations, e.g. Chejara, Joharī, Manihār, Lohār, Zulāhī, Kāgdī, etc. These castes, as such, were chiefly occupational in character.[2]

It has been cogently argued that in pre-colonial Indian "Kingdom" or semi-autonomous state, the idea of the ruler was intimately connected with the political structure of the kingdom or state; one could not exist without the other.

Political events impacted dramatically on royal portraiture. There were hundreds of states within the Indian subcontinent, each with its own ruler and his ministers, with its own laws, its own currency and its own local traditions and customs. Most of the states had their indigenous school of painting too, whose skilled artists delighted in figurative work, including portraits of royalty.

Naïve artists sometimes made the ruler twice the size of other figures in the painting, to emphasise his importance. Indeed, there is often more in these portraits than we can appreciate today at first glance, because the symbolic meanings of costumes, jewels, crown, swords, furniture, animals and other props have been lost in the course of time.

By the 1750s the patronage of artists by the Mughal emperors was in decline. With the weakening of the central authority these artists had to seek patronage elsewhere. But behind the surface glitter, there was a sense that real power was passing from the rulers. Artists were among the first to feel the effects and many of them were forced to look for a livelihood elsewhere. Many went to provincial courts, whose rulers were freeing themselves. The arrival of artists bringing different skill and techniques with them led to vigorous new schools of painting, that acknowledged existing indigenous tradition but added with Mughal flair and craftsmanship. Court artists continued to work where they found patronage, but they could not remain unaffected by the new ideas, even if they still produced traditional painting themselves. It was in the last decade of the sixteenth century that English merchant ships first began to reach India and the East India Company was establishing its factories around the Indian coastal areas. During Jahangir's reign, an English officer was granted permission for starting business in the city of Surat, in the year CE 1611 and gradually, they spread their business establishments all over India.

Apart from the merchants and officials of the company, various other European travellers and adventurers made their way to India and they observed with close insights into Indian events and ways of life, some of them committed to paper in the form of travel memoirs. Among those some were more inclined than others to commission pictures that would either illustrate the subject matter of their writings or reflect their interest in Indian environment. Some of the travellers were painters also. Such European paintings were so popular that huge amount of copying went on; and it soon became fashionable for ruler and rich men to employ European artists.

In the wake of the company officials, also came the artists whose paintings were to change the face of portraiture irrevocably. The mystique of royalty, the physical space that distanced them from the public, has vanished, the halos have gone, and the ruler is now seen to be ordinary people, standing before the viewer in intimate engagement.

By CE 1800 artists were producing a large number of paintings which portrayed either single or group figure. They made drawing of craftsmen — goldsmith, blacksmith, potters, of workmen such as bricklayers, carpenters, water-carriers, or of familiar bazaar figures such as dancing girls, peddlers, shopkeepers, *pherīwālā*, shoe-maker, and many types of holy men, both Hindu and Muslim. They depict festivals, hook-swinging and

Hindu and Muslim weddings. Drawings by these artists were hawked around the bungalows of the British and also sold at the ghats when the ferry-boats halted on their way up and down the Gaṅgā River.

During the period (1750–1860), several families of artists were running bazaar shops. Some were done on paper, and others were done on mica or glass and ivory. By middle of the nineteenth century the most successful shops were run by big artists, they were not only skilful painters but good businessmen also. They marketed their paintings in big cities and sold the paintings in sets according to the subject.

But, painted in oil or watercolour or drawn in sepia or pencil, the painting of this period revealed a pathetic Indian scenario. The painful countenances, faces without smile, blank looks, figure pervaded with nervous tensions are enough evidences to prove visually the economically deprived people, shaky, panicky, unstable and unaware of their future. The paintings depict the saga of a struggle for subsistence and survival.

References

1. *Indian History Congress* 1987, 47th Session, p. 270.
2. *Indian History Congress*, 1981, 42nd Session, pp. 326 and 331.

5

Social and Political Condition of the Country

It was an eventful period that witnessed the end of Muslim rule, the rise and fall of Marāṭhās and the foundation of British Empire in India. The period began with political disintegration leading to struggle for power, not only among the Indian states but also between the European trading companies in India. This chaotic political situation facilitated political indulgence of foreign traders.

The beginning of the Mughal Empire and the eventual demise can be traced back to the reign of Aurangzeb in the late seventeenth century. Taking a broad view of the state of things at the death of Aurangzeb, it is difficult to ignore the facts that in spite of the brilliant qualities of head and heart which enabled the emperor to extend the Mughal Empire over the whole of Deccan and south India, the grave defects of his character are mainly responsible for the sudden collapse of the mighty empire which then included nearly the whole of India and Afghanistan. Mughal Empire reached the highest point only to break down, and Aurangzeb must share both credit and discredit for the same, at least to a very large extent. But it was not merely the fall of an empire but also the end of an epoch which ushered in a period of decline and distress after a century of peace and prosperity — under the strong and wise governments of three generations before Aurangzeb. Peace and security "the sole justification of Mughal Empire" no longer existed in India at the time of Aurangzeb's death. Aurangzeb was not a political genius and lacked the qualities of a true statesman who could initiate a policy and enact laws for moulding the life and thought of his contemporaries as well as of future generations. He could realise the futility of his work before his death.[1]

The eighteenth century was a tragic period in the history of India. The later Mughal rulers had neither the ability nor strength of character to pilot the ship of the state properly and political unity which the great Mughals had managed to maintain in some form or other for about two centuries disappeared under their effeminate successors exposing the country to various disintegrating forces. The nobility, some of whose predecessors had served as worthy pillars of the state under Akbar or Shahjahan, had utterly degenerated, and with regrettable unscrupulousness bartered away the interests of the country for sordid personal gains. These maladies naturally caused a breakdown of administration and decay of sound governance, and a veritable insolvency reduced the country to a state of ruin in all respects. Thus, devoid of internal strength it excited external aggressions, which produced highly devastating effects. It also emboldened the European trading companies to convert India into an arena of bitter political conflicts which ultimately resulted in giving a new turn to the destiny of India in various ways.[2]

As the empire disintegrated, local elites and communities sought, and in many cases were able to obtain, more autonomy and control over their own affairs. Each region had a different experience in the aftermath of empire, however, not only politically but also economically with some reigns faring far better than others. The events in Bengal were specially wrought with significance for the subsequent history of the subcontinent, for it was there that the Britishers first obtained an extensive foothold within the internal affairs of the erstwhile empire, with an account of the European trading companies, whose long-term effect on Indian history was so disproportionate to their numbers and even to their immediate impact on the era from 1750 to 1857.

The political condition of Bengal at that time was extremely unstable. In the great days of the Mughal Empire, provincial governors had been immediately responsible to the court at Delhi, but as the power of central government declined this system of direct control broke down. The Mughal governors of Oudh, Bengal and Deccan freed themselves from the control of central government and the state rulers found the time opportune for assertion of their independence. The European trading companies dabbled in Indian politics. The Mughal emperor had become the shadow of a great name, the Marāṭhās had not yet recovered from their defeat at Panipat by Afghans and there was a vacuum waiting to be filled.

Although the development of British power in India was a continuous process from the middle of eighteenth century, the temptations which prompted the European traders to interfere in the politics of the Indian powers were very strong and not easily resisted. Affairs were also taking a serious turn in the country.

The increasing disintegration of Mughal Empire became marked after 1720 and was conducive to the growth of English settlements in Bengal and on the Coromandel Coast. The growth of the three presidencies was well marked during the period from 1708 to 1746. Madras was fortunate to secure the grant of some suburban villages and exempted the company goods from customs duties. In Bengal the English power grew up steadily in strength and prosperity. The Nawāb of Bengal granted to East India Company the right of free trade only on payment. His successors — Suja Khan (1725-39) and Ali Verdi Khan (1739-56) — respected it. On Ali Verdi Khan's death in 1756, the Company officials were more concerned with the doings of the *nawāb* than with other activities. On 23 June 1757 took place one of the decisive events in Indian history. Subedār of Bihar, Bengal and Orissa Nawāb Siraj-ud-Daula found himself deserted as well as betrayed in the battlefield by his traitor general Mir Jafar. The Nawāb discovered that he was the victim of a conspiracy, leaving the field to the Britishers as victors and the Britishers got an undeserved victory at Plassey.

British success at the Battle of Plassey in 1757 marked a decisive upswing in the East India Company fortunes and the Battle of Buxar in 1764 confirmed the decision of Plassey. Now English power in northern India became unchallengeable. The whole territory up to Allahabad lay at their feet and road to Delhi open. Never after Buxar did the *nawāb*s of Bengal or Oudh ever challenge the superior position of the Company. If the Battle of Plassey had made the Company a powerful factor in the politics of Bengal, the victory of Buxar made them a great power of northern India and contenders for the supremacy of the whole country.[3]

It is also noteworthy that for a long time the East India Company never acted in its own name. It always did it with some local chief in order to advance its own interest. Thus the Company established its position in the south by supporting the claims of the *nawāb* of Carnatic. Similarly, in Bengal, it acted in the name and under the authority of the Nawāb of Murshidabad. Even after the Company became the virtual ruler of Bengal, it did not claim sovereignty. Lord Clive approached the Emperor for the grant of *dīwānī* rights and for decades the Company acted as the agents of the Emperor. The Governor-General of East India Company described himself as the servant of Shah Alam, the Emperor of Delhi. In this way the appearance of the sovereignty of the Emperor was kept up. The people of India did not, for a long time, realise how the Company was gradually becoming the real ruler of the land.

By the 1820s, the East India Company had demonstrated its military strength against every potential contender, and established its supremacy over the whole of India. The "Subsidiary Alliance" system was used by Wellesley to bring Indian states within the orbit of British political power. The system played a very important part in the expansion of the Company's dominions and many new territories were added to the Company's possessions.[4] From the British point of view, Lord Dalhousie's (1848-56) rule is full of important events in every field, his contribution to the building up of the British Empire in India is very great. If there had occurred any possibility of annexing an Indian state, Dalhousie would not have missed it. Some important Indian states were annexed by the enforcement of the Doctrine of Lapse, i.e. Punjab, Oudh, Satārā, Jhansi and Nagpur. Whatever might have been the facts, the Indian states undoubtedly believe that the existence of all native principalities was threatened and extinction of all states was regarded to be a question of time only.[5] In fact, Dalhousie's Doctrine of Lapse was a part of his imperialist policy and his British mentality wanted to tear the mask of Mughal sovereignty and dispose of Indian princes who pretended to be descendant of the Mughals.

This came to many people as a shock. They realised that from being mere traders or agents of the emperor, the East India Company had, in fact, become the ruler of vast territories of India. The growing discontent was aggravated by Dalhousie's policy by which he incorporated into British territory one state after another.[6] When the people saw that Indian states were being liquidated one after another and landlords were being eliminated as a class, it came as a great shock to them. They felt that the Company was at last showing its true colours and seeking to change the very structure of Indian social and political life. All these had a cumulative effect and made the people aware of the change in the status of the Company. The shock of the discovery created a great disturbance in their minds and affected not only the civil population but also members of the armed forces.[7]

In the light of the available evidence, we are therefore forced to the conclusion that the uprising of 1857 was not the result of careful planning nor was there any mastermind behind it. What happened was that in the course of 100 years from 1757 to 1857, the Indian people developed a distaste for the East India Company's rule. Since the company had at first acted in the name of the *nawāb*s/Emperor, Indian people did not realise that power had been captured by a foreign race, and they had been reduced to the position of slaves in their own country. Once this realisation became widespread, the conditions were created for an outburst. This, when it took place, was not due to the conspiracy of a few individuals or groups but to the growing discontent of large numbers of people.[8]

The growth of the British power in India has perhaps no parallel in history. It was not a case of outright conquest of a country by another, but a story of slow penetration in which the people of the land themselves helped the intruders. The fact, that the intrusion of the British into India was not in the name of the crown, helped to conceal the true nature of their activities. If the British crown had from the beginning taken any direct part in Indian affairs, the Indians would have realised that a foreign power was entering the country. Because East India Company was a trading company, they did not think of it as a potential ruler. It also enabled the agents of the Company to behave in a way in which no agent of the crown could have done. The agents of the Company had no such scruples. They bowed to the pettiest officials with the same readiness as any Indian trader. They indulged in bribery and corruption without any fear of being pulled up by their own ruler.

The record of the East India Company had been of ever-increasing conquest and commercial exploitation. The greed of perfidious Britishers knew no limits. The pace of conquests and annexations had quickened in the generation that preceded the rising of 1857. The Indian princes nursed grievances against the East India Company which has usurped their positions. The people had not been reconciled to the rule of the East India Company. The resentment of the Indians had found expressions in a number of insurrections from time to time in different parts of the country;[9] to mention only a few — the Bareilly rising of 1816; the Cola insurrection of 1831-33; the Santhal rising of 1855-56, etc. The simmering discontent burst out into a violent storm in 1857.

The great uprising of 1857[10] is generally described as the Sepoy Mutiny. Almost all the books dealing with the struggle represent it as a rebellion of the Indian Army against the so-called constituted government of the day. The subject has sought to interpret the events of 1857 in other ways. It may, however, be pointed out that the only legal title of the East India Company was to act as the agent (*dīwān*) of the Mughal Emperor in revenue matters in respect of Bengal, Bihar and Orissa. The territories East India Company had since acquired were by military conquest but nowhere had the company challenged the suzerainty of the Emperor. When the Army denied the authority of the Company, it appealed to the Emperor to resume his sway. It is, therefore, a debatable point if the revolt of the Indian Army can be regarded as a simple case of mutiny against the sovereign of the land.

About the nature and character of the rebellion, historians have held divergent views. It has been painted as "a mutiny" confined to the army which did not command the support of the people at large. The interpretation is unsatisfactory. Even the army as a whole did not join the revolt, and a considerable section fought on the side of the Company. The rebels came from every section of the population and enjoyed the support of the masses. In the trials of 1858-59 thousands of civilians along with the soldiers were held responsible for the rebellion and were severely punished. The struggle was suppressed with great violence and for many years there was an atmosphere of terror in the country. Hundreds of innocents were executed without any trial. There was hardly any region in northern India where corpses hanging from gibbets, did not remind the people of the vengeance of the Britishers. No Indian dared at that time to speak or write freely about the events of 1857.

If the Indians were guilty for the murder of European women and a few cases in children, the record of the British was equally tarnished by dark deeds, which were no less heinous and barbaric than those of Indians. From Benares to Allahabad there was hardly a single tree which was not used as a gallow for unfortunate peasants.[11]

The incident of 1857 proved that these attempts had not met with the desired result. Common life had developed among Hindus and Muslims a sense of brotherhood and sympathy which enabled them to resist the indoctrination of 100 years. That is why the struggle of 1857 took a national and racial turn but not communal. In the fight for freedom, Hindus and Muslims stood shoulder to shoulder. Their common effort was to liberate themselves from the British yoke.[12]

Throughout all these changes, armed rebellion against foreign rule is an emotive outcome and the revolt that began in the Indian summer of 1857 is especially compelling. There is enough unity across creeds to fight *firaṅgī* rule and the factions within a fractured imperial family. The 1857 resistance in Delhi anchored around the last Mughal emperor Bahadur Shah II. Six months in the life of city from 11 May (when last Mughal emperor accepted the rebellion) to 7 October (when the Mughal emperor left Delhi on his way to exile), the royal houses were abolished following the war of independence.[13]

In 1857 all powers formerly held by the East India Company were transferred to the British crown.[14]

References

1. Jadunath Sarkar, *Fall of Mughal Empire*, in 4 vols., New Delhi, 1950 & 1966.
2. B.L. Grover and R.K. Sethi, *Studies in Modern Indian History*, New Delhi, 1963, pp. 1 & 8.
3. For detailed study, see R.C. Mazumdar (ed.), *The Maratha Supremacy*, vol. VIII and *British Paramountcy and Indian Renaissance*, part 1 and 2, Bharatiya Vidya Bhavan, Bombay, 1963; B.L. Grover and R.R. Sethi, *Studies in Modern Indian History*, New Delhi, 1963; C.B. Ashor and Taibote, *India Before Europe*, New York, 2006, pp. 284-86; *Indian History Congress*, 38th Session, 1977, pp. 474-79.
4. Percival Griffith, *The British Impact of India*, London, 1912, pp. 78, 82-83, 89-94.
5. During the rise and expansion of British dominion in India, the East India Company from time to time had given assurances that not only the rights and privileges of the Indians but their laws, habits, customs and prejudices would be respected. The right of adoption has

always been a great religious ceremony and greatly prized by the Hindu. Lord Dalhousie broke with precedents and was on many occasions guided by imperial considerations. Some titular sovereignties were swept away. The regal title was abolished.

By the middle of nineteenth century the British opinion in India was ripe for annexation. In fact, British imperialists believed that Britain alone had the capacity for good government, the Indians had to be governed. *The London Times* had given expression to the same sentiment when it referred to the Indians "as the very small people" which "a very great people has gone across the earth and taken possession of." (B.L. Grover and R.R. Sethi, op. cit., p. 155).

6. Percival Griffith, op. cit., pp. 99-101.

7. The effect of the dissolution of the Kingdom of Oudh was the greater as a large proportion of the soldiers in the Bengal army was drawn from this area. They have served the Company faithfully and been one of the major factors for extending its sway in different parts of the land. They suddenly realised that the power which the Company had acquired through their services and sacrifice was utilised to liquidate their own king. I have little doubt in my mind that 1856, when Oudh was annexed, marked the beginning of a rebellious mood in the army generally and in Bengal army in particular. It was from this time that they began to think that the Company's rule must be brought to an end.

8. We can get an idea of the situations as they existed in the thirties of nineteenth century from a study undertaken by a distinguished British Civilian of the day. The Hon'ble Frederick John Shore was the son of Sir John Shore and served in various capacities in the Police, the Revenues and Judicial department in the north-western region of the Bengal Presidency. He contributed a series of articles anonymously to the *India Gazette*, one of the Calcutta daily papers, and later in 1837 published them in book form under the title, *Notes on Indian Affairs*. Shore has left us in no doubt about his appraisal of the public mind. He has repeatedly pointed out that even though outwardly everything was clam, the situation was charged with dynamite and it needed only a spark to start a violent conflagration. It was this simmering discontent which ultimately broke out in the outburst of 1857.

9. Sabyasachi Bhattacharya (ed.), *Essay in Modern Indian Economic History*, Delhi, 1987, p. 249.

10. Vinayaka Damodar Savarkar, *1857 Kā Swātantrya Samar* (in Hindi), New Delhi, 2007, p. 42.

11. Gurumukh Nihal Singh, *Landmarks in Indian Constitutional and National Development (1600-1919)*, Benares, 1933, p. 100.

12. Hirendra Nath Mukherjee, *India Struggles for Freedom* (A History), p. 51.

13. At one point in time, dispute about whether it was triggered by fear of religious pollution or if it was accurate to call it a "War of Independence" dominated historical writings. A significant corpus is also concerned with social and economic reasons that welded sepoys and peasants, local notables and the ordinary urban populace together.

    The rebellions arrive in Delhi in May. The breathless and brutal pace of actions craftily combined with insights into the religions and class elements underlining it. While elite-poets, jewellers, moneylenders were ambivalent about joining the uprising, it were the weavers and textile merchants who were among its most "enthusiastic insurgents."

14. Justin MacArthy, *History of Our Own Times*, vol. III.

    This article is at present in the collection of India Office Library, and it was published in Britain on 13 October 1857. It is as below —

    "Your (Englishmen's) conduct has all along been mean and pettifogging. You accuse our ancient Mughal rulers of despotism. They were despotic to some extent; but on the whole, they knew how to govern an empire — you know how to keep a shop. They had a large mind; you have an ingenious and a crafty one. They could conceive of grand projects. Despite their faults, they were loved by a grand people like us. They settled in the country and tried to improve it. Your servants come here only to make money and go home as soon as they have satisfied themselves on that score. Indeed, inasmuch as we have come to know you, we have learnt to despise you. With increasing knowledge we have known that the Anglo-Saxon race is selfish and hypocritical in the extreme and always unprincipled in matter of gain."

6

Socio-Economic Condition of the Country

INDIA'S strength rests upon the principle of the unity of man, the unity of thought and the unity of spiritual experience. India lives today because, in spite of centuries of degeneration, these principles have been kept alive in the national consciousness. Cultural patterns have, of course, been modified from time to time, but different environments, diversified racial contributions, and innumerable local and historical traditions have not basically affected the continuity of Indian culture.

The eighteenth century was a period of transition in Indian history, politically as well as economically. It was also marked by growing social insecurity and demoralisation, prejudicial to the interest of the people. But the social structure in general was marked by the traditional features, and some new ones added to these age after age according to the special environments or influences of each. Some of these may have become decadent and static with the march of time, and the evils caused by the disorder and confusion of the eighteenth century were, no doubt, gnawing at the vitality of our existing traditions.

India lived in her villages and agriculture was the very backbone of her economic life. The Indian village was a self-sufficient unit. In time of normal rainfall it produced sufficient foodgrain for its subsistence. Other needs of the people were met by village artisans. The village communities were little Republics, having nearly everything they needed within themselves, and almost independent of any foreign relations. They seem to last where nothing else lasts. Dynasty after dynasty tumbles down; revolution succeeds revolutions, Hindu, Muslim conquerors and Muslim kings, Mughal, Marāṭhā, Sikh, Europeans are masters in turn, but the village communities remained the same. In time of trouble they arm and fortify themselves; a hostile army passes through the country; the village communities collect their cattle within their walls, and let the army pass unprovoked, if plunder and devastation be directed against themselves and the force employed be irresistible, they flew to a friendly village at a distance, but when the storm has passed over, they return and resume their occupation. If country remains for a series of years the scene of continual pillage and massacre, so that the village cannot be inhabited, the villagers nevertheless return whenever the power of peaceable possession revives. A generation may pass away but the succeeding generations will return. The sons will take the place of their fathers, the same site for the village, the same position for the houses, the same lands will be reoccupied by the descendants of those who were driven out when the village was depopulated and it is not a trifling matter that will drive them out, for they will often maintain their post through the times of disturbance and convulsion, and acquire strength sufficient to resist pillage and oppression with success.

There was well-regulated caste

polity for due enforcement of caste rules over individuals and maintenance of effective social control over them. This "caste authority" served to preserve social order and morality to a great extent in all parts of India. Family system, which formed the chief agency for social relationship, was mainly patriarchal in character, except in few provinces and among some primitive communities in comparatively backward areas. Marriage was a common social practice for all; and marriage meant a sacred bond for a happy conjugal life according to its established laws.

Caste had much influence in determining the vocational professions of men. In general, whatever be the trade of the father, the same is that of a son; the caste system helped specialisation in arts and industries. Probably due to the rapid administrative and economic changes in the country since the middle of the eighteenth century, professional arrangements strictly on caste groups were becoming loose gradually within certain limits.[1]

Indian society is mainly based on religion. Most of the social activities derive their sanction from religion. Hinduism is, in fact, a socio-religious way of life. Therefore, the misinterpretation of and degeneration in religion was bound to have its repercussions on the social plane, on the institutions and the customs of the Hindus. The medieval concept of society was based on the idea of status. This led to development of a well-graded hierarchy in social life with definite privileges, rights and functions in the form of the caste organisation. An individual's caste was determined by birth, this made the caste system rigid. The condition of women was very miserable, for they were kept indoors, and in seclusion. The practice of child marriage was very common. As widows, they lived miserable lives. The sale of girls, *satī* system (widow-burning) were some of the typical evil customs prevalent in Indian society. Polygamy prevailed among the society. These and other harmful customs were, no doubt, the result of an all-round degradation of the life of the people of India in eighteenth century.

The contemporary pattern of Indian culture is a confluence of various cultural streams that have been flowing into India ever since the dawn of her history. The Indian cultural pattern has expanded and grown richer with the passage of time, this was due to its adaptive characteristics which made assimilation and accommodation of obtruding cultures possible. For instance the impact of the Western civilisation in no way upset the ancient course of Indian history. The waves of Western civilisation dashed over the firm rock of Indian culture. No doubt, a few loose rocks were swept away in the new tide, but they were only carried away and could not get a foothold on the soil of India.

Further, India had always enjoyed a sense of unity — both in a geographical and cultural sense. Her bonds of unity were more real and true than those derived from the national sentiment, for these bonds that united India were the heritage of the past. The sense of unity, common intellectual heritage, traditions and social life led to the development of a vague idea of nationality. The establishment of our places of pilgrimage in the four corners of India indicates that our ancestors did not lack the conception of one nation.[2] And this conception "fired the people with an idea of nationality, in a manner unknown in other parts of the world." This feeling of nationality was still latent and had not taken a definite or a conscious form; nevertheless it lay dormant, and out of it was developed a sense of national consciousness. This conception of nationality did not influence the thought and action of the men in a deep and all-pervading manner. It found a clear expression occasionally in individuals, and in groups at times of stress or provocation.

The educational system of a country has a considerable influence in moulding its society. In the sphere of education the old centres of learning with international reputation had disappeared in course of time under the influence of adverse forces. But in other ways the traditional features prevailed. Elementary education was widespread. There were institutions for it in urban as well as rural areas, and it was encouraged in almost every stratum of society. Generally, in the institutions for primary education, teachers were appointed and students were admitted irrespective of caste or creed. The general features of elementary education were similar in different parts of India, with some differences in detail. Thus, they became acquainted with such matters as were needed for a common civic life, not so complex as that of today, and higher virtues of life were also inculcated into their minds.

In the eighteenth century India's political destiny did not only take a new turn, but there were also weighty changes in various phases of her economic life. The quickly succeeding political revolutions in this country, which completely disintegrated the old order in government and administration, were existing at the same time with the rise of some new forces which vitally affected the economic life of the people subjecting them to the manifold evils of an ill-adjusted transition.

For many years, historians believed that the economic benefits were arising from political unification with the Mughal Empire. But peaceful travel and trade became difficult, local economics were disrupted by recurrent warfare, and the misery of the common people deepened. The eighteenth-century India has been considered an era of political anarchy and economic recession, a kind of dark Age ushered in by the collapse of the Mughal Empire. The notion of an economic breakdown accompanying political disorder was promoted by the East India Company, which justified its growing involvement in internal Indian affairs during the late eighteenth century on these grounds.[3]

A close look at the economic picture reveals considerable variation from region to region. The area that suffered most from the decline of Mughal power were the farmer hubs of the diffused, but closely intermeshed, imperial economy. The Agra-Delhi corridor was the first to be affected, due to the Jat insurrections.[4] The large numbers of merchants and weavers had fled from Agra for safer surroundings, and a foreign trader travelling to Agra needed maximum guards for his protection. As internal struggles for power broke out at court after Aurangzeb's death, the Sikhs of the Punjab revolted and Marāṭhā power grew up in western and central India. Traders travelling from Agra to Surat were victims of the repeated attacks by peasant bandit-armies at large. As a result, Surat bankers refused to issue *huṇḍī*s for Agra, and consequently the foreign trading company closed its trading post. The Punjab, one of the wealthiest provinces of India, was also badly affected by the events of the eighteenth century. The Marāṭhā homeland in the western Deccan witnessed an expansion of agricultural cultivation. Agriculture was extended in eastern Rajasthan as well.

The English might not yet have had a major impact on India in the early eighteenth century, India had become far more important to them. Their trade with India not only led to huge profits and considerable political power for those in the East India Company, but it was also a source of national pride. The nature of their export trade had also drawn the English into far more involvement with the internal economy of India. Unlike raw materials, textiles were a manufactured commodity that went through a complicated and lengthy production process involving spinning, weaving, washing, dyeing and printing. The Europeans were entirely dependent on Indian intermediaries for the procurement of goods.

A large inland trade was maintained efficiently by organised caravan and river-borne traffic. A network of the inland trade in foodgrains was in the hands of *bañjārā*s who moved from one part of the country to another in bullock convoys and also catered to the requirements of armies on the march. The European armies in the eighteenth century also depended upon them for their supplies.

The cities in India did not develop to be the homes of a new middle class in society. Most of the trade and crafts were confined to the production and exchange of weapons of war and luxury goods for the nobility. The village community, isolated and self-sufficient, continued to be the central feature of Indian life, and cities were parasitic, hollow, agglomerations. If a section of the nobility and the small but wealthy class of traders who catered to the needs of princes and courtiers had undertaken to collect together groups of craftsmen in the towns and set up a large and organised farm even of cottage industry, we might have seen in India prototypes of the "free town" of Europe; we might have seen something like the social revolution which the Europeans brought about in their own interest; we might have been spared the sight in our country of a tragically immobile society. That, however, was not to be. The wheel of production in myriad villages moved with uncanny monotony from age to age. Whatever was surplus was enjoyed by the small and exacting class of exploiters. The state normally spent a minute proportion of its revenues on irrigation and public works and devoted the rest to the maintenance of expensive apparatus of administration, and to the refinements of luxury in which the few elite indulged.[5] The majority of India's people lived at a low enough level of subsistence. Real, decisive progress was thus at a discount, for while spectacular prosperity was not often visible, society in general became derelict and for the overwhelming majority economic processes remained (ante-deluvian) out of date.

All the wars, invasions, revolutions, conquests, famines, strangely complex and destructive as the successive action in India may appear, did not go deeper than its surfaces. The East India Company/England has broken down the entire framework of Indian society, without any symptoms of reconstitution[6] yet appearing.

The English merchants in India encountered a people whose military organisation was weaker and weapons more antique. More important, they knew at home a more advanced productive system and were therefore very much better equipped for the contest. Feudalism had virtually made its exit in Britain, and her economic structure was correspondingly stronger. The British were the first conquerors superior in essential respects and therefore above the lures of absorption or semi-absorption into the receptive texture of India's society.[7]

The British intruders, therefore, broke up the Indian handloom and destroyed the spinning wheel, dissolved the foundations of Indian life by wrecking the village communities, and "by levelling all that was great and elevated in the native society." They set up a new and avid landlordism, and uprooted the union between agricultural and manufacturing industry.

The Indian technology, when the British encountered it, was by no means primitive, but was unprogressive, and was bound up with a social order hostile to its development. Industrial skill in India, in the sense of a knowledge of the properties of minerals, metals and vegetables and of the technique of using them, was very far from rudimentary. One thinks at once of textiles — calicoes and silks, muslins, numerous varieties of them, and so amazingly fine. Indian steel was the material used for the famous Damascus blade. Huge iron columns at Delhi and Dhar prove the ability of Indian craftsmen to forge the metal into larger masses than European foundries could negotiate before nineteenth century.

The British conquest shattered the traditional basis of Indian economy and remained a foreign force, operating from abroad and drawing an enormous tribute. Its work was, in the beginning and for quite some time, only a work of destruction. India was directly exploited by the foreigners and colossal fortunes were transmitted overseas. The British manufacturer employed the arms of injustice to keep down and ultimately strangle a competitor with whom he could not have contended on equal terms, though the competitor had already been struck down and bled in thousand wounds.[8]

The decisive wrecking of the Indian economic structure took place with even more drastic form after 1813. The misery hardly finds parallel in the history of commerce. So in 100 years of protected warfare after the Battle of Plassey (1757), Britain reduced India to submission.[9]

Although it is literally true that the rule of the East India Company had ended in 1857, the fact nevertheless remains that it gave place really to the rule of the British Empire. How the whole of the political organisation in India was merely a cover for the protection of the British mercantile interest in this country, is to be seen from the fact that though India seemingly is subject more to, yet she really suffers less from, the rule of civilians, than bankers, shipping magnates, railway companies and various manufacturers and merchants, exporters and importers.

We have thus endeavoured to show how, almost in every branch of Indian administration, the British people and the English government merely lend cover to trade and industries using their power, authority and influence for the furtherance of British interest in India.[10]

References

1. R.C. Mazumdar (ed.), *The Maratha Supremacy*, Bombay, 1977, pp. 755-56.
2. *Indian History Congress*, 38th Session, 1977, pp. 489-90.
3. B.L. Grover and R.R. Sethi, *Studies in Modern Indian History*, New Delhi, 1963, pp. 1ff.; Kali Kinker Datta, *Survey of Indian's Social Life and Economic Conditions in the Eighteenth Century (1707-1813)*, Calcutta, 1961, Introduction.
4. Vincent A. Smith, *The Oxford History of India*, 3rd edn., London, 1958, pp. 575-76.
5. Ashar C.B. & Taibote, *India Before Europe*, New York, 2006, p. 186.
6. Ibid., pp. 275 ff.
7. B.L. Grover and R.R. Sethi, *Studies in Modern Indian History*, New Delhi, 1963, p. 8.
8. Romesh Dutt, *The Economic History of India*, vol. II, In the Victorian Age 1837-1900, Delhi, 1963, pp. 21, 91-92.
9. Prithvi Singh Mehta, *Bihāra — Eka Aaitihāsika Digdarśana* (in Hindi), Patna, 1940, pp. 302, 305, 314, 335, 347-48.
10. K.S. Shelvankar, *The Problem of India* (Penguin), p. 146.

    The British trader in India got an unexampled opportunity when disorder and unsettlement followed the fall of Mughals, and with alacrity they said it. They were supported by their own government who saw in them the instrument for realising capitalistic ambitions which the Industrial Revolution in England had opened up before their eyes. On Indian soil, they had their own system of forts, had all there was to be learnt about intrigue and coercion, and for over a century they have waged by hook and by crook a struggle for concession and monopolies. They now increased their intervention in local tangles, especially in Bengal and Madras, the Gangetic Delta, and by theft, bribery, confiscation and merciless taxation squeezed money and goods out of the people with a ferocious rapacity that has hardly a parallel in history. They soon come to discover how much more profitable sovereignty was than mere trade, "and like a tiger that had tasted blood pursued the hunt for territory with a new zest until, in the end, the whole continent lay under its dominion."

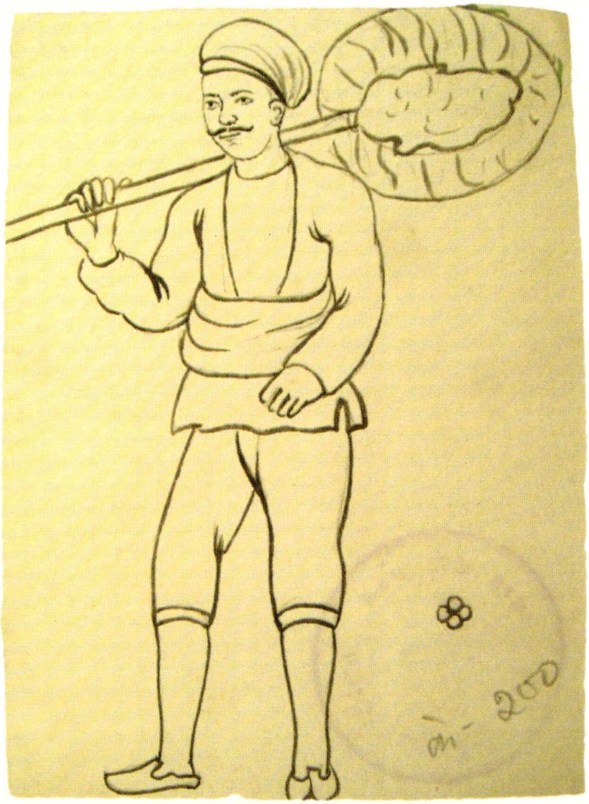

fig. 1. A man holding fan (*paṅkhā*), paper, water colour (Acc. no. 12065).

fig. 2. A man with swan, paper, water colour (Acc. no. 12063).

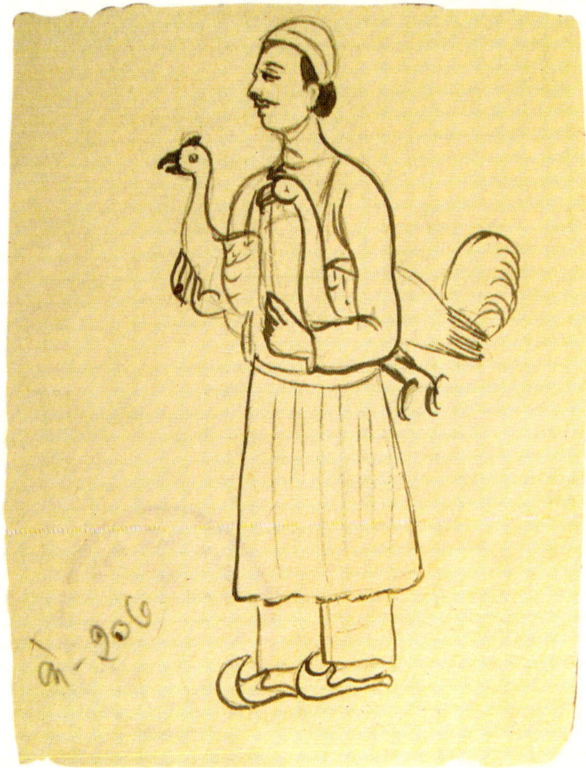

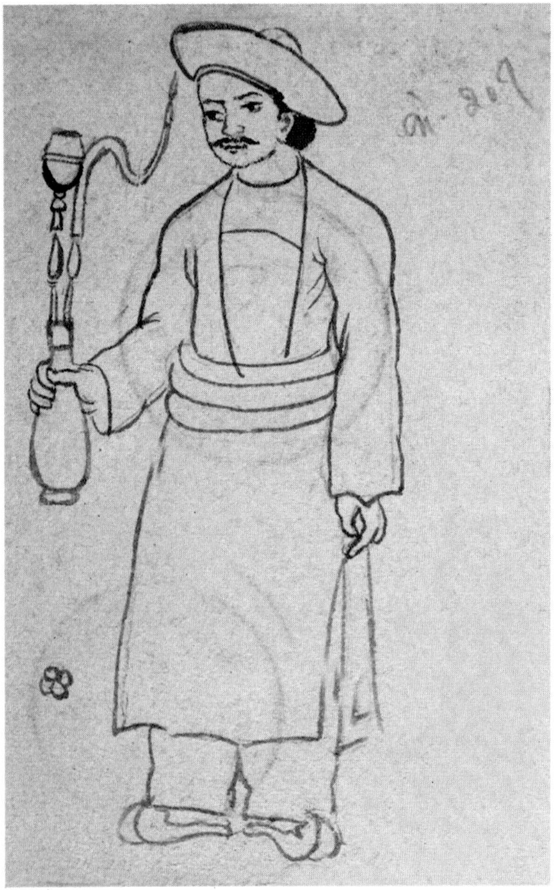

fig. 3. Hukkā-bearer, paper, water colour (Acc. no. 12060).

fig. 4. Hukkā-bearer, paper, water colour (Acc. no. 12061).

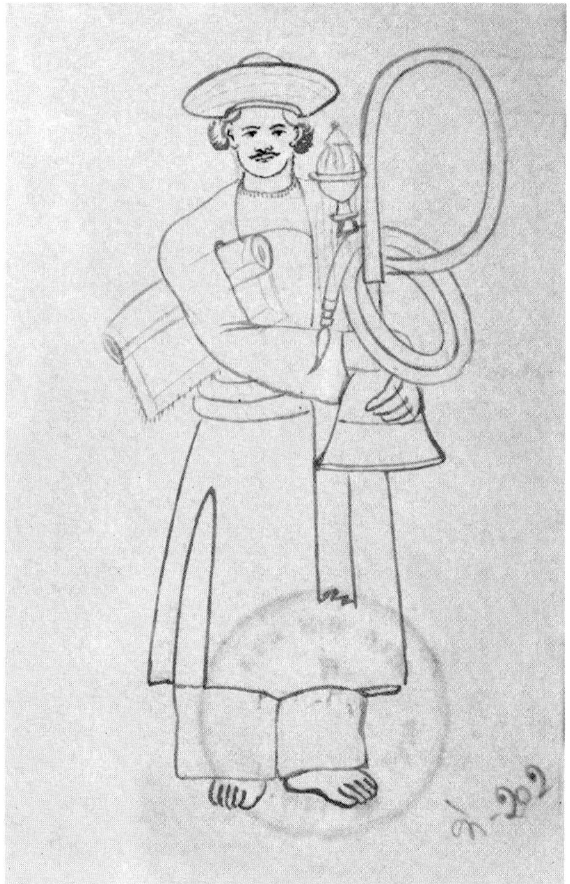

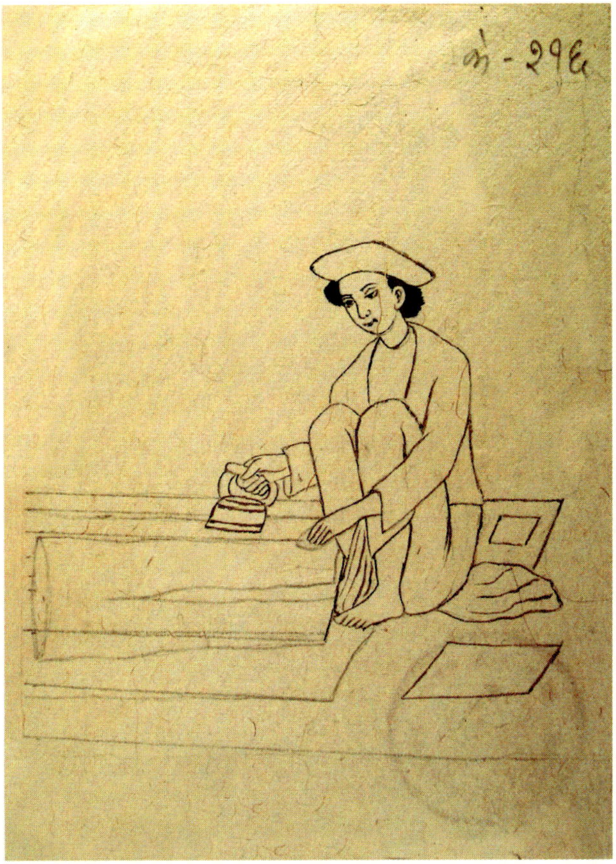

fig. 5. Washer-man (*dhobī*),
paper, water colour (Acc. no. 12059).

fig. 6. Musician (playing with *sāraṅgī*),
paper, water colour (Acc. no. 12031).

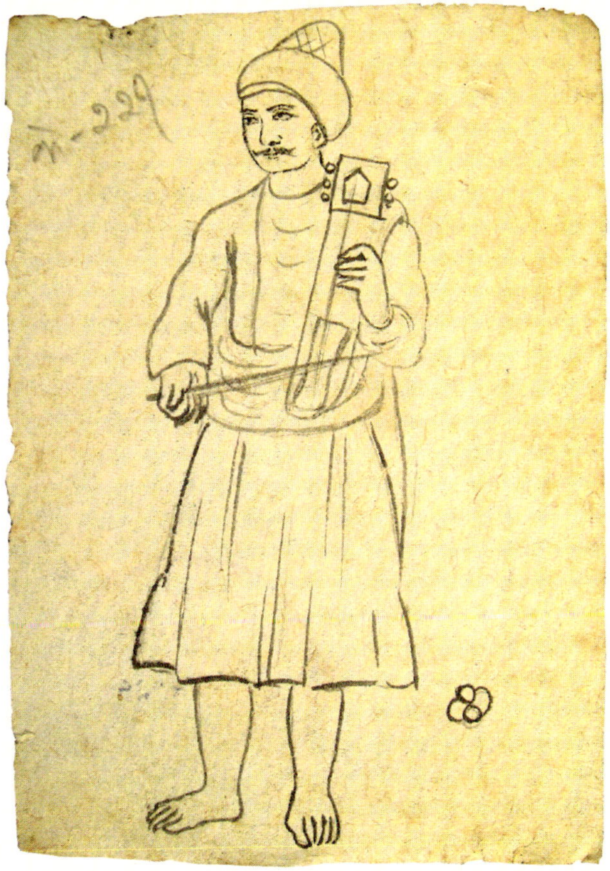

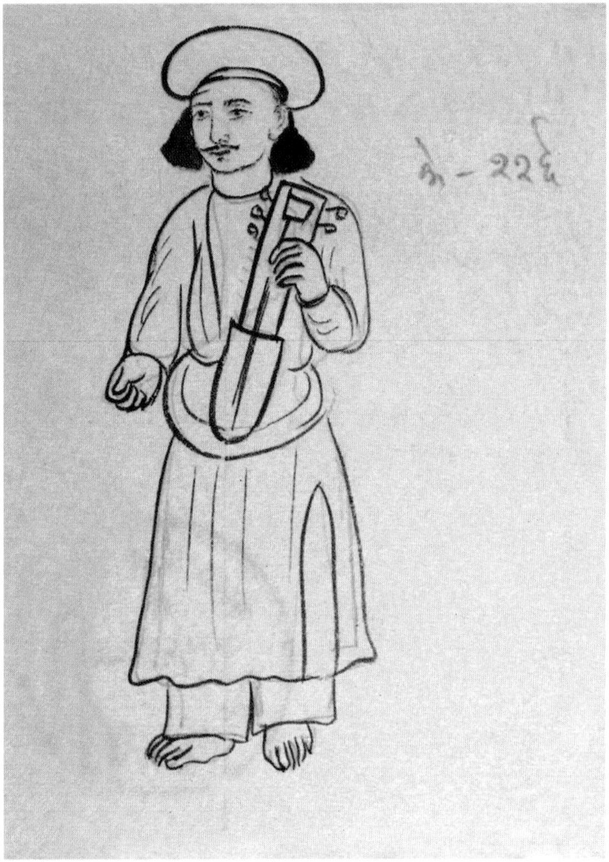

fig. 7. Musician, Paper (Acc. no. 12075).

fig. 8. Musician
(playing with *ekatārā*) (Acc. no. 12033).

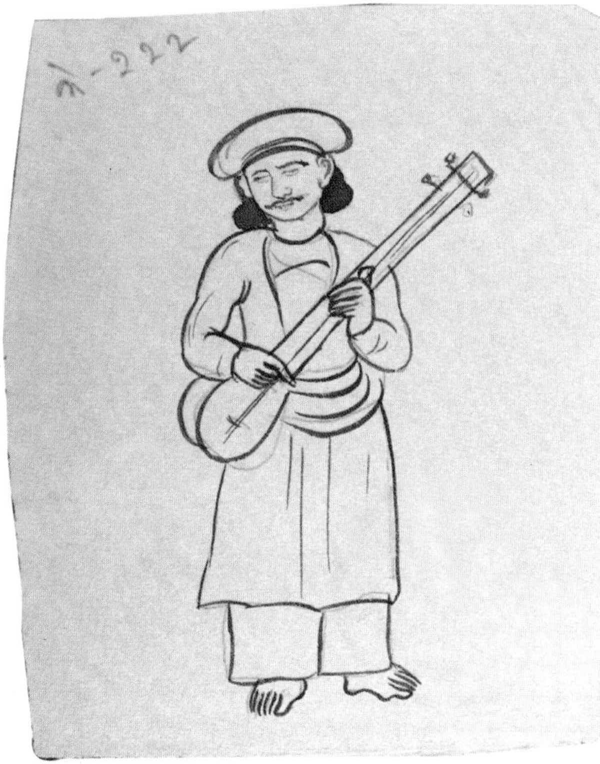

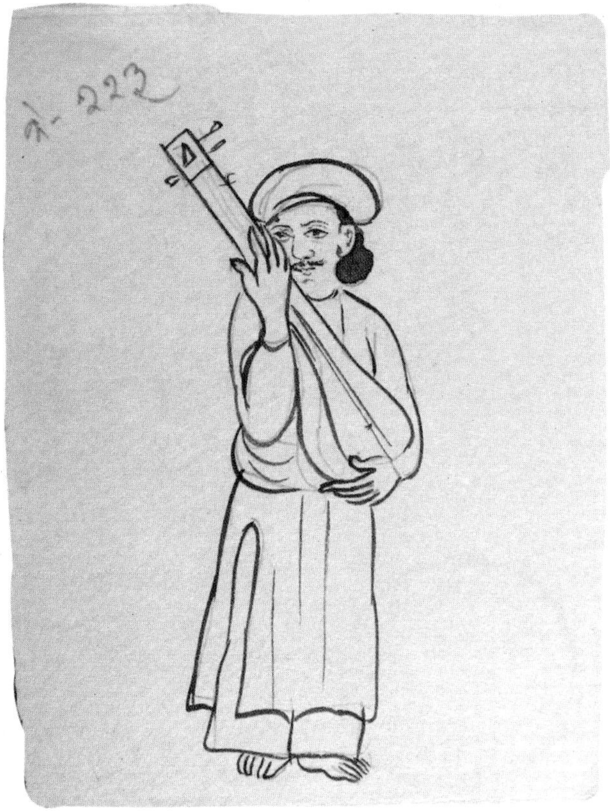

fig. 9. Musician (playing with *ekatārā*) (Acc. no. 12034).

fig. 10. Drummer (*ḍholakiyā*), paper (Acc. No. 12035).

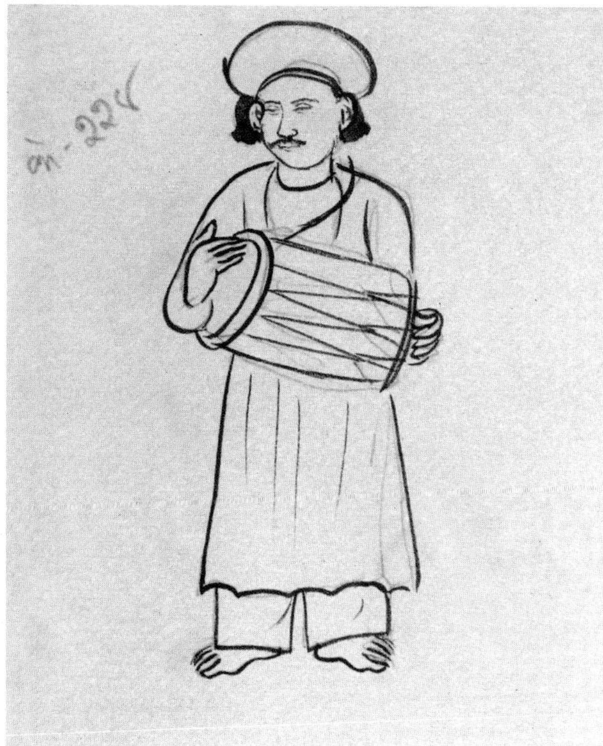

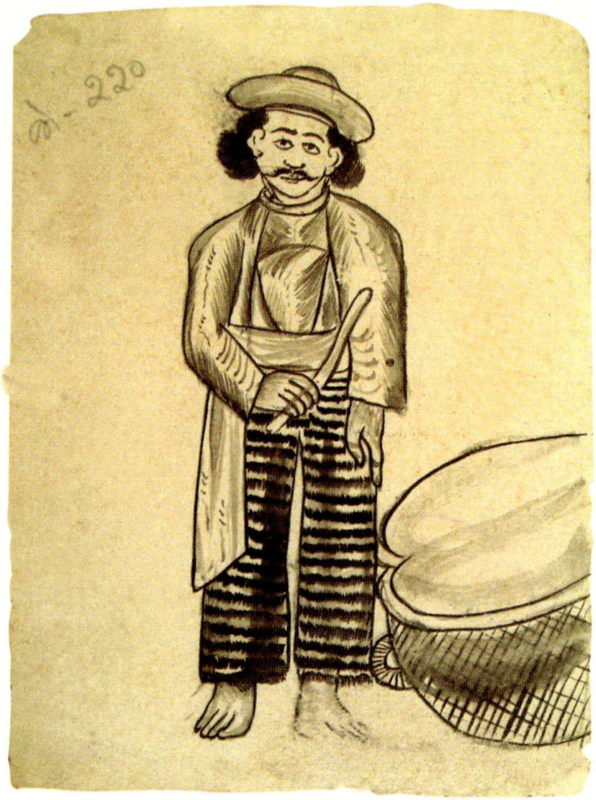

fig. 11. Drummer (a person with drumstick) (Acc. no. 12066).

fig. 12. Drummer (Acc. no. 12076).

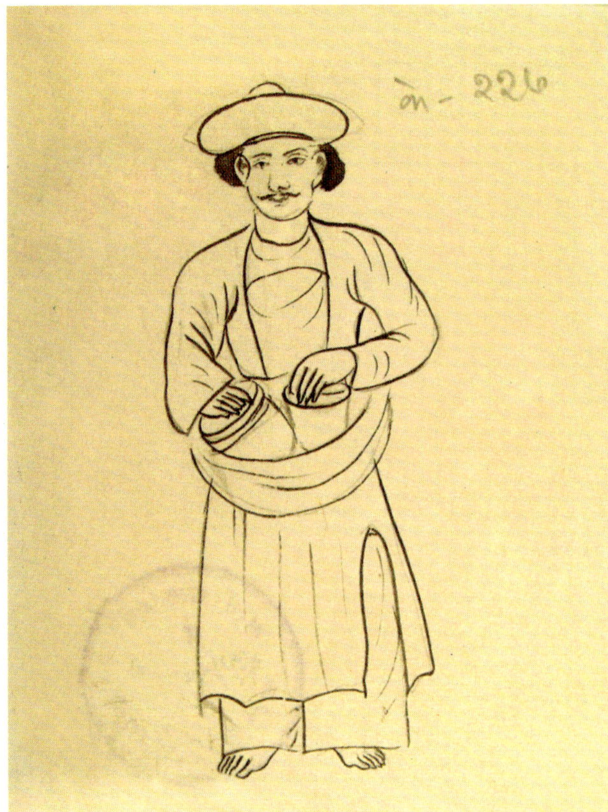

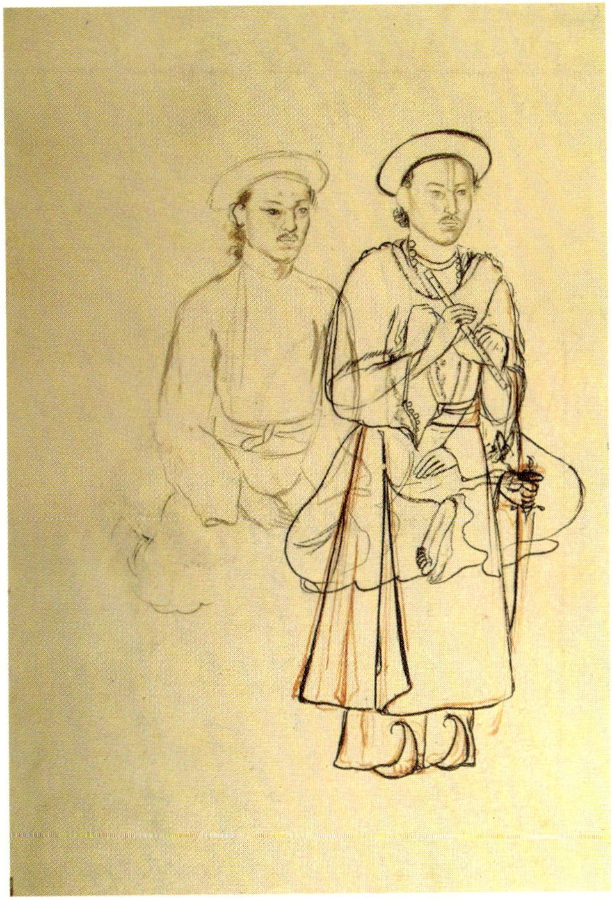

fig. 13. Flute Player (*bāṅsurī-vādaka*).

fig. 14. Vocalist (*gāyaka*) (Acc. no. 12074).

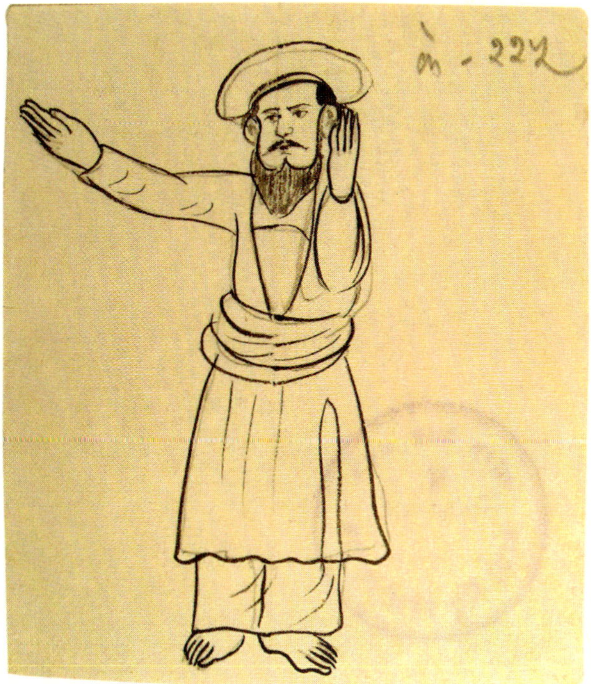

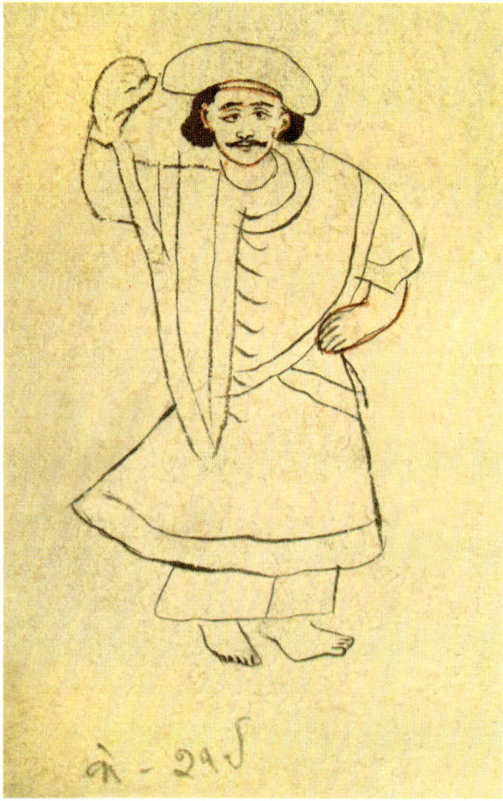

fig. 15. A man in dancing posture (Acc. no. 1643).

fig. 16. Punjabi confectioner (*halavāī*), paper, line drawing (Acc. no. 1682).

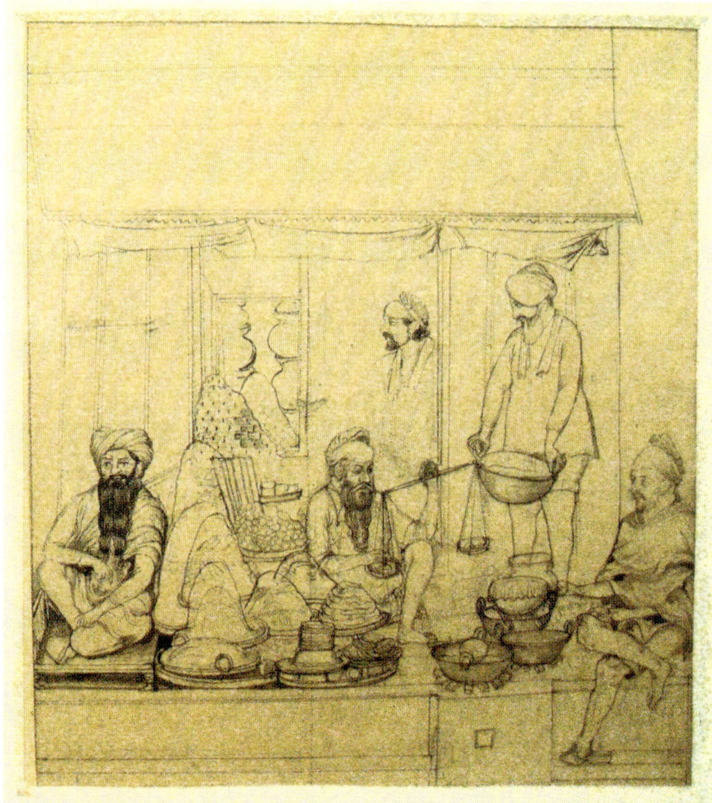

fig. 17.A labourer, paper, Line (ink) (Acc. no. 12030).

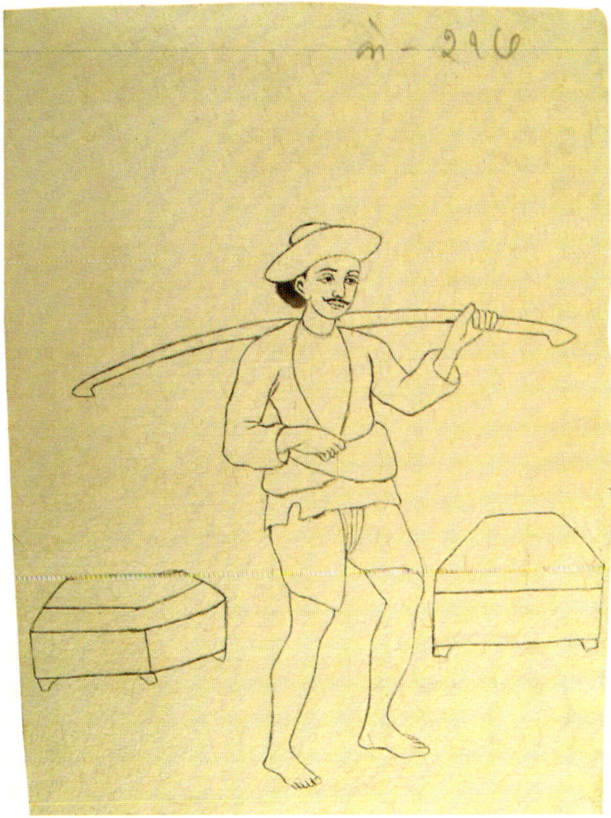

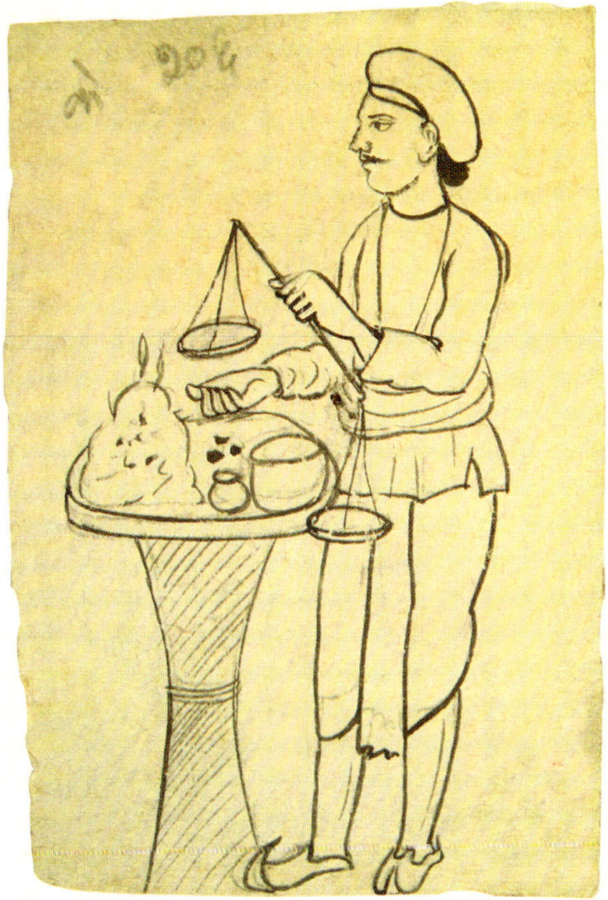

fig. 18. A vendor (*khomacāwālā*), paper, line (ink) (Acc. no. 12028).

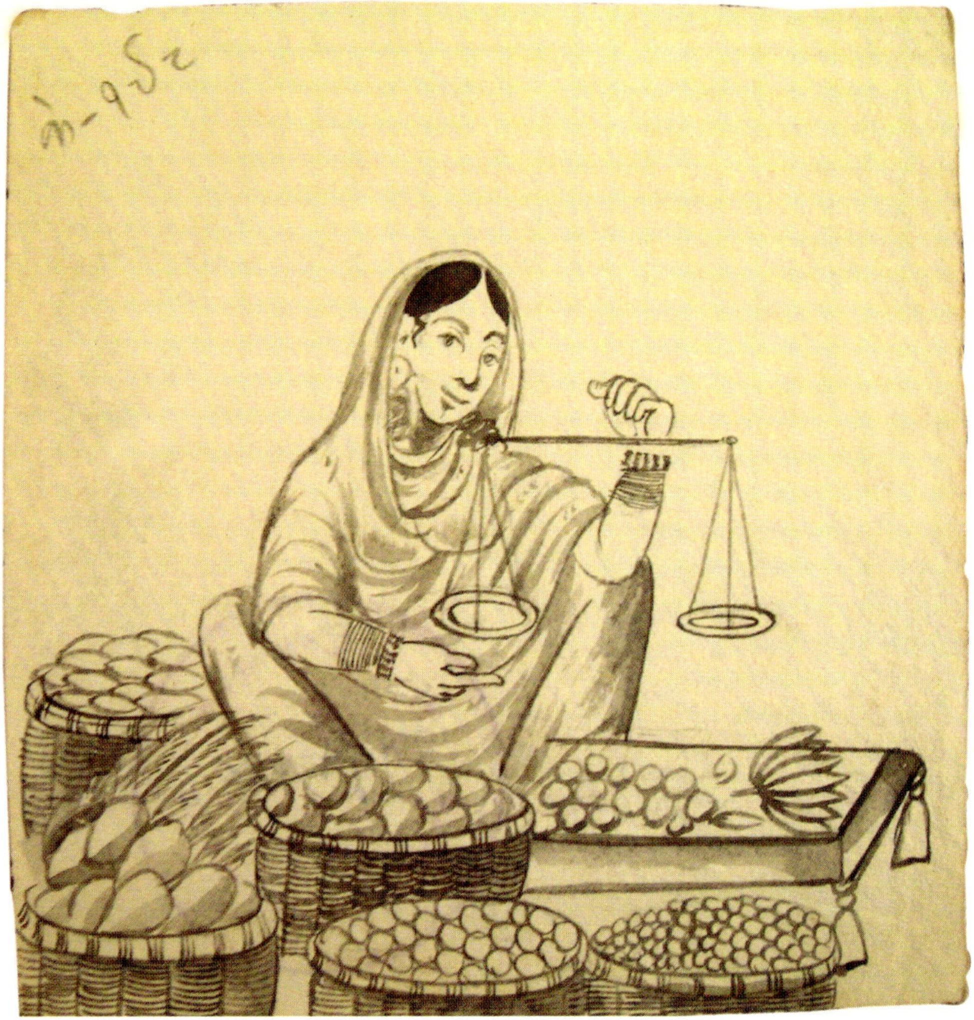

fig. 19. A female selling fruit, paper, line (ink)
(Acc. no. 12024).

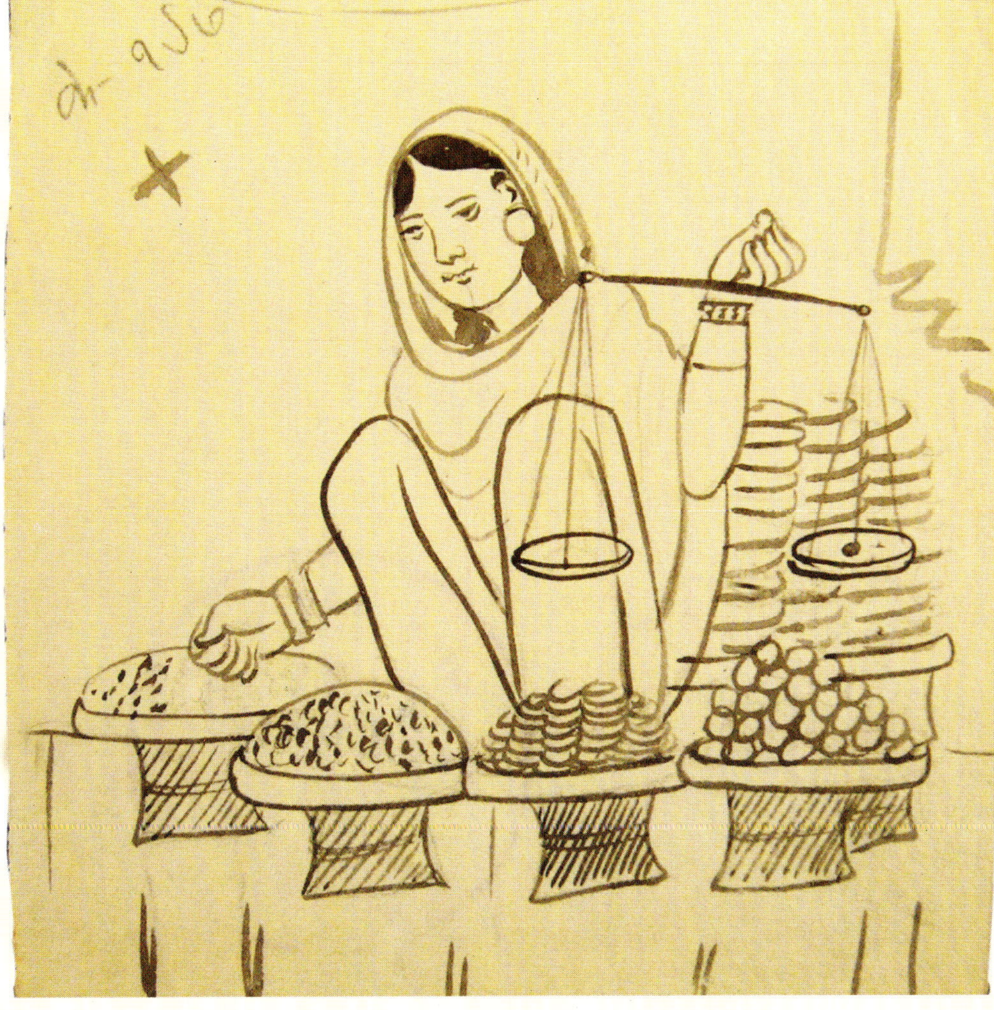

fig. 20. A female selling sweet, paper, line (ink)
(Acc. no. 12025).

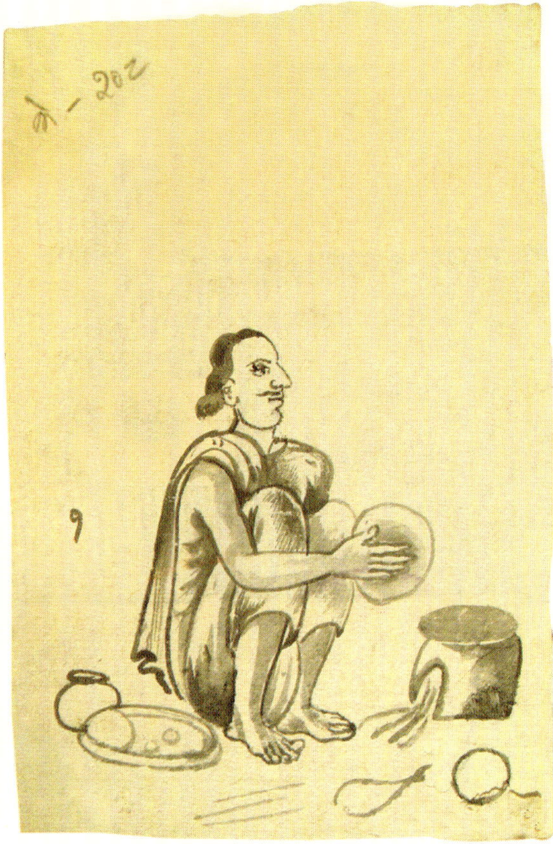

fig. 21. A man is baking bread (*chapātti*), paper, line (ink) (Acc. no. 12056).

fig. 22. Barber (*nāī*) (Acc. no. 1681).

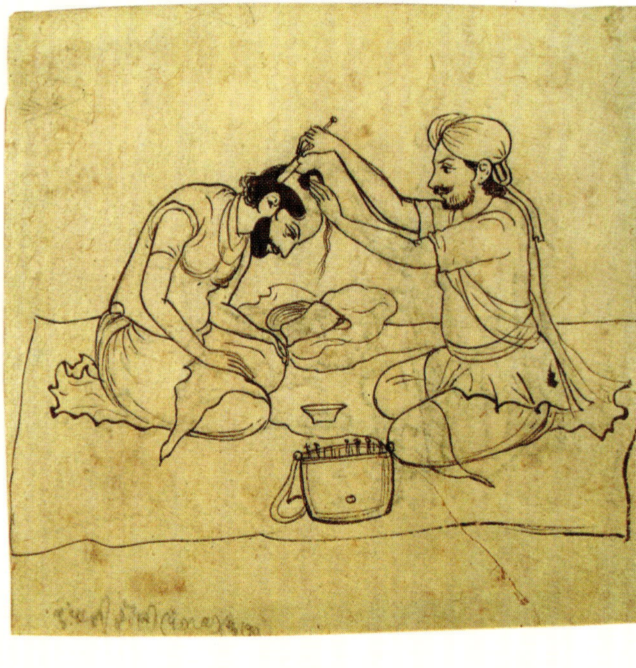

fig. 23. A female spinning cotton into, paper, line drawing thread (Acc. no. 1647).

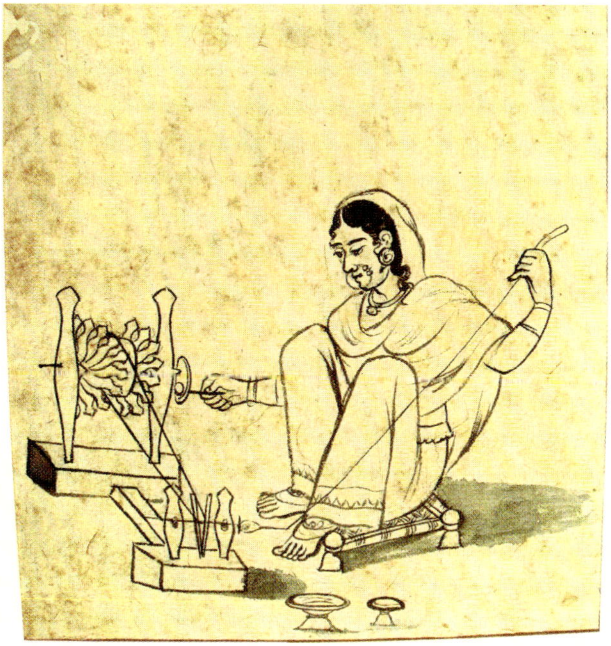

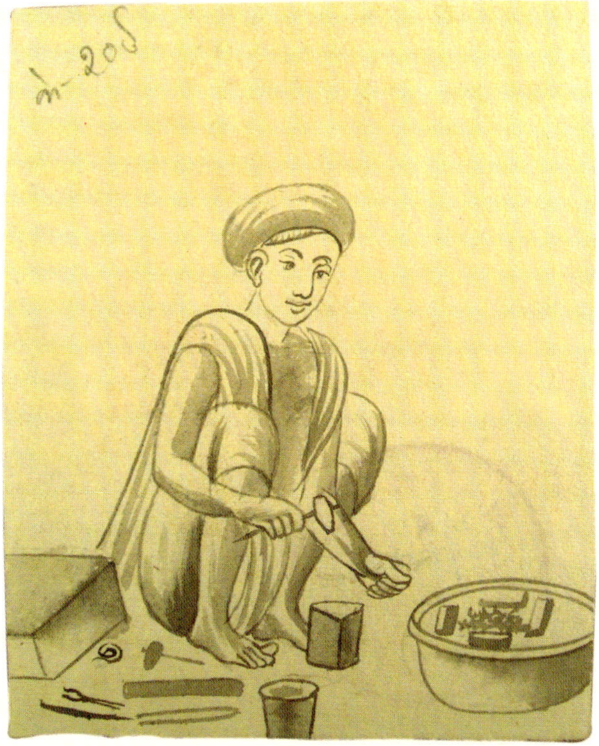

fig. 24.Goldsmith (*sunāra*), paper, water colour (Acc. no. 12057).

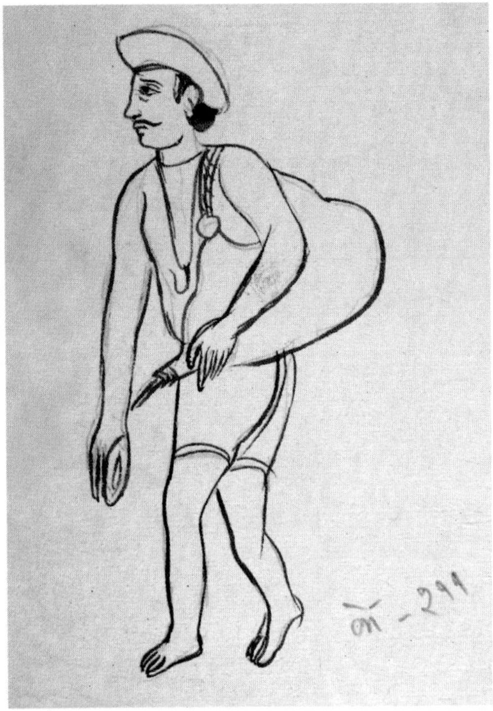

fig. 25. A person carries water (*bhiśtī*), paper, line (ink) (Acc. no. 12026).

fig. 26. A man with dogs, paper, line (ink) (Acc. no. 12027).

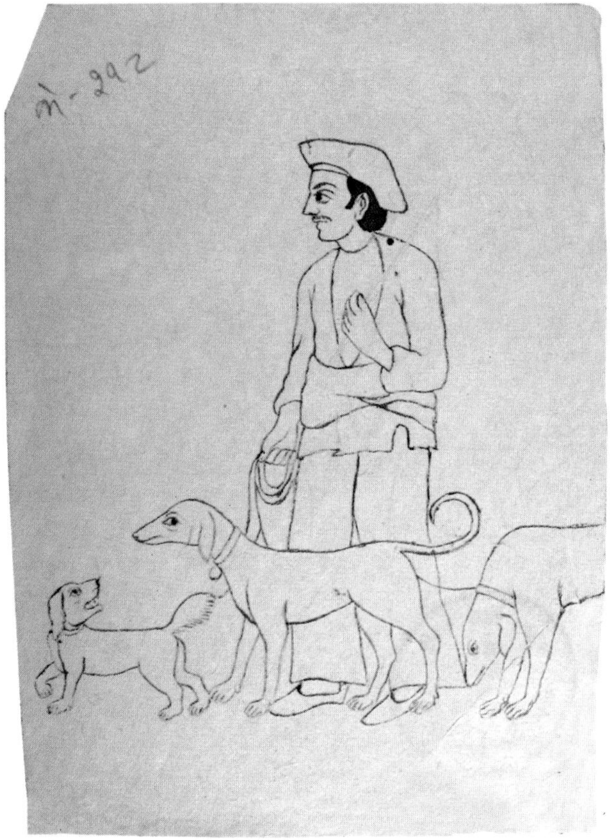

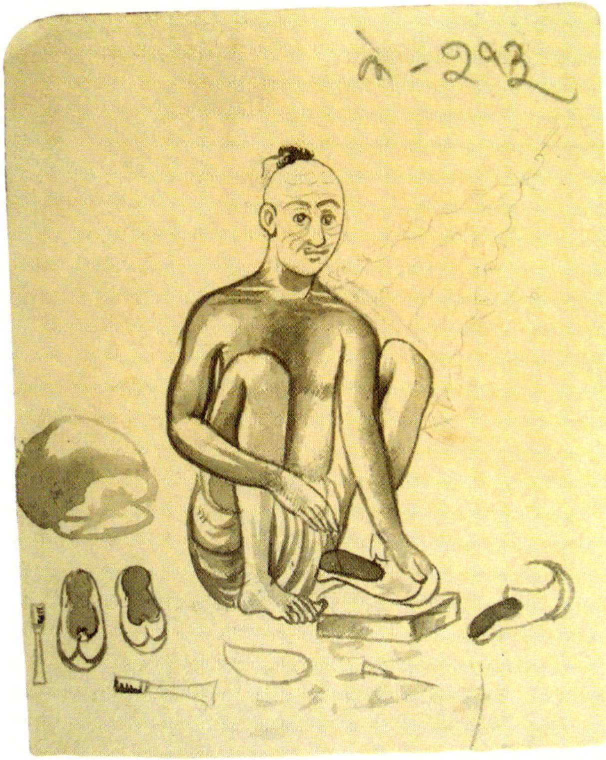

fig. 27. Cobbler (*mocī*), paper, line (ink) (Acc. no. 12022).

fig. 28. A man polishing the shoe, Paper, line (ink) (Acc. no. 12029).

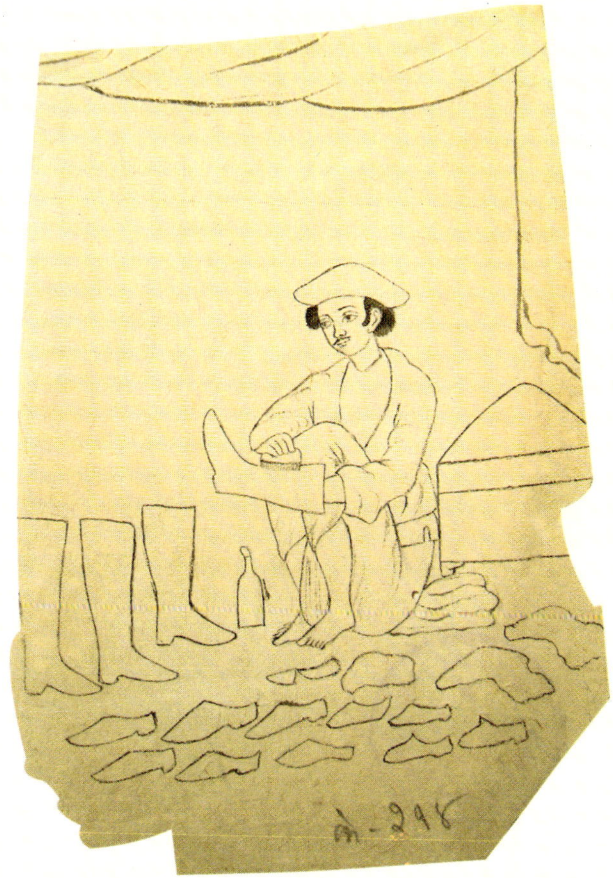

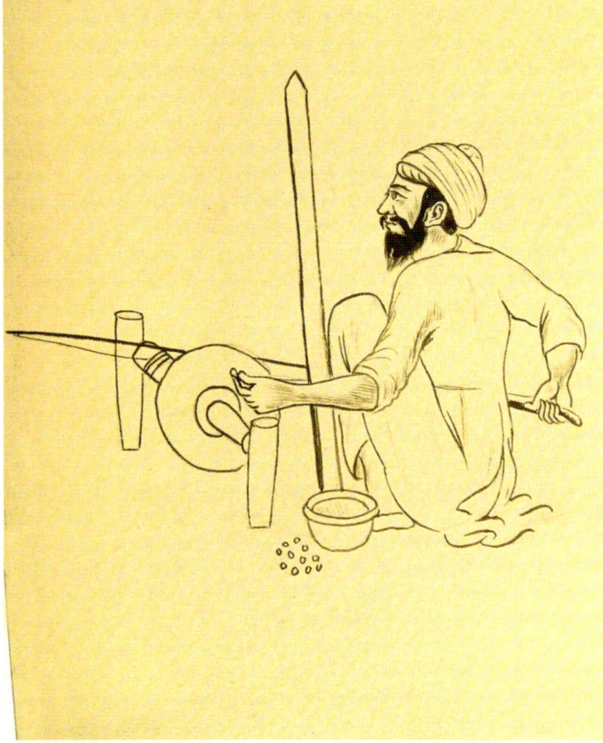

fig. 29. A man polishing stone (gem), paper, line (ink).

fig. 30. Potter, paper, line (ink).

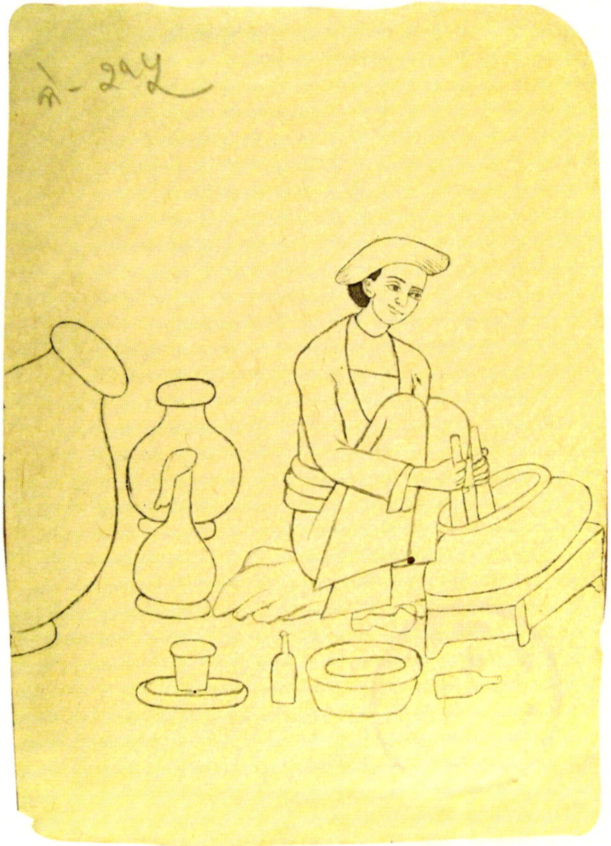

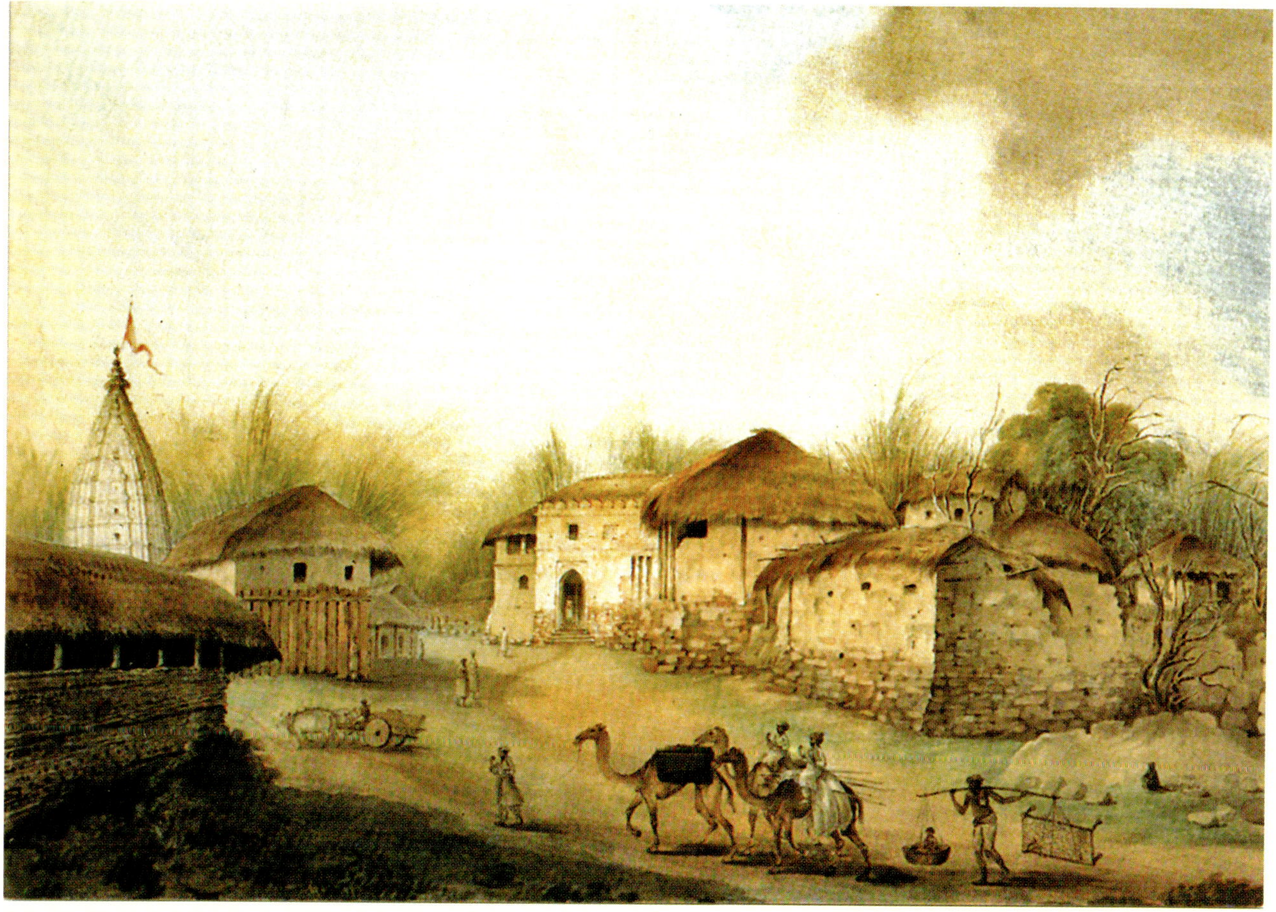

fig. 31. House and a temple, paper, water colour.

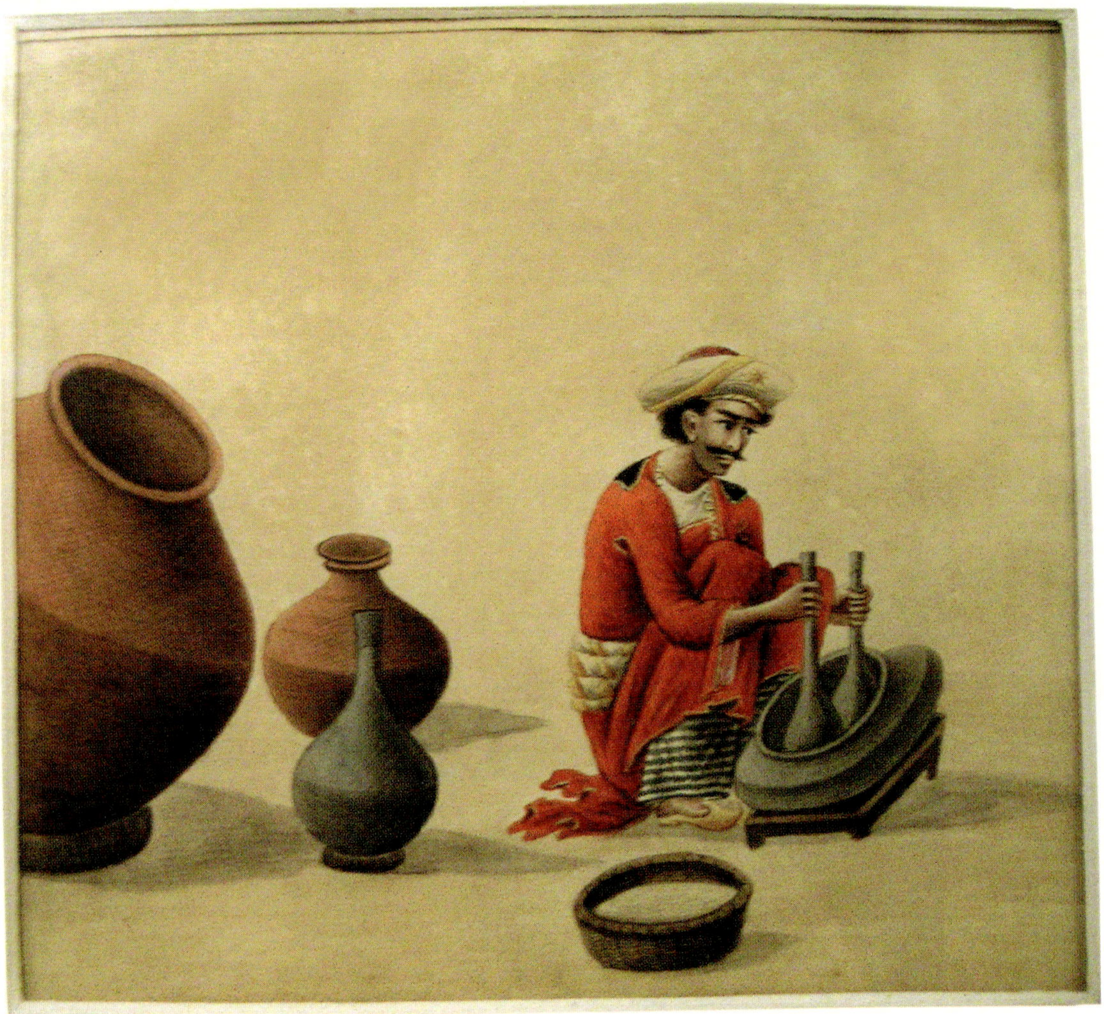

fig. 32. Potter (a person who makes clay pots) (Acc. no. 10572).

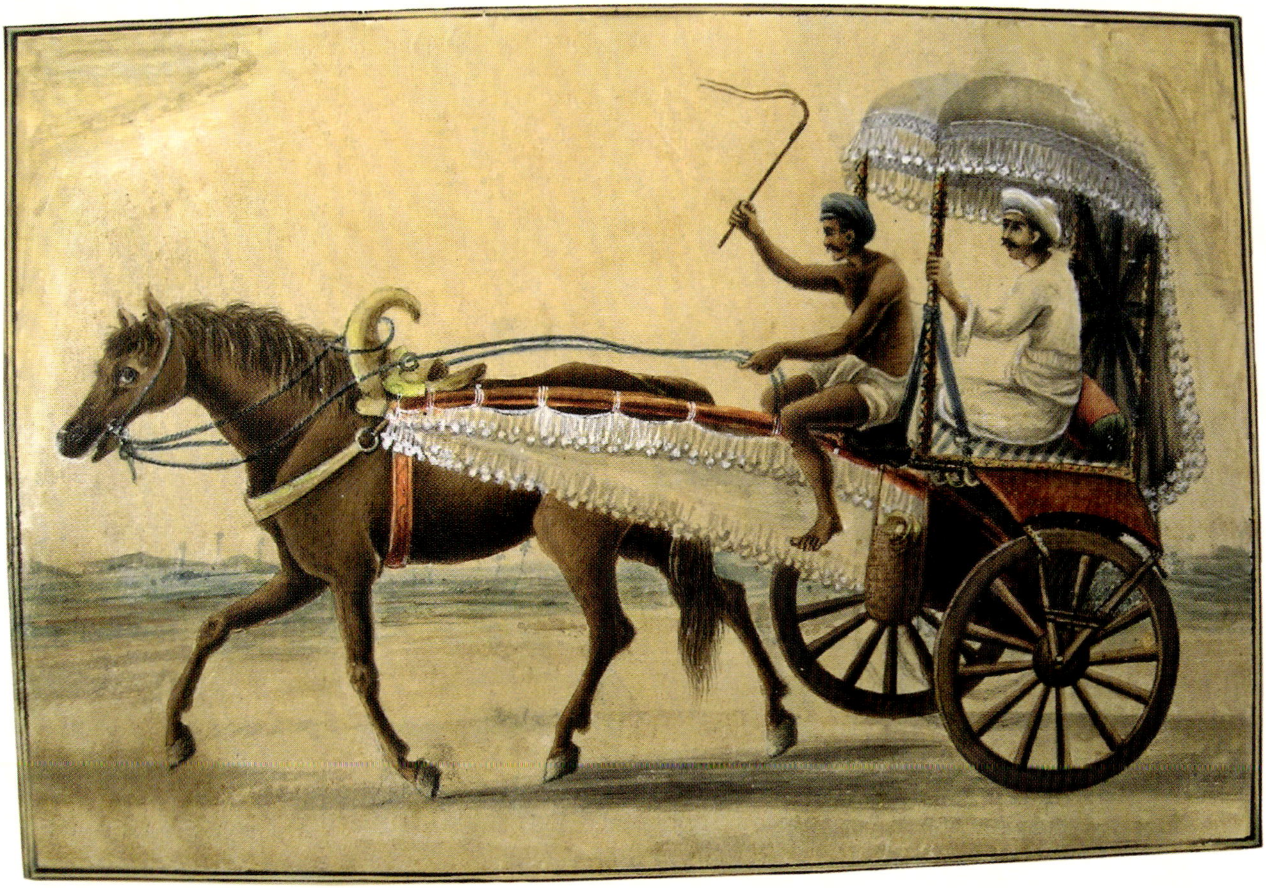

fig. 33. *Akka* (Horse cart), paper, water colour (Acc. no. 1574).

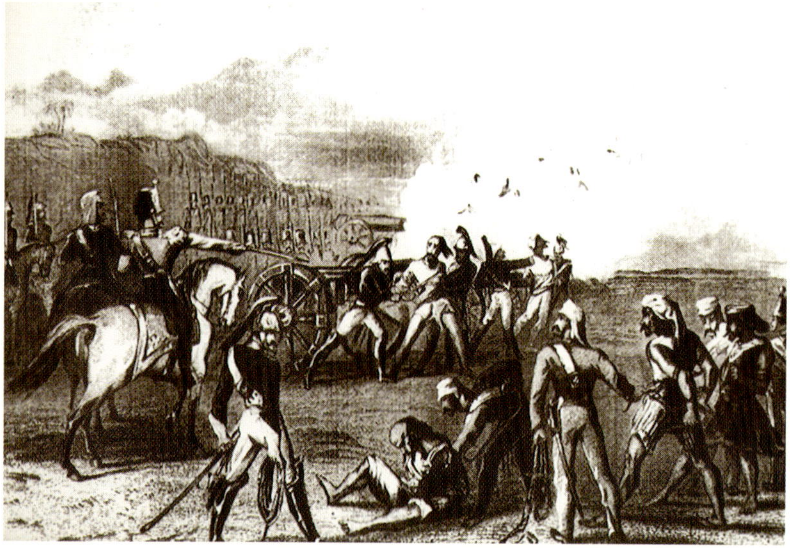

fig. 34. Blowing Indian soldiers from gun in 1857, lithoprint.

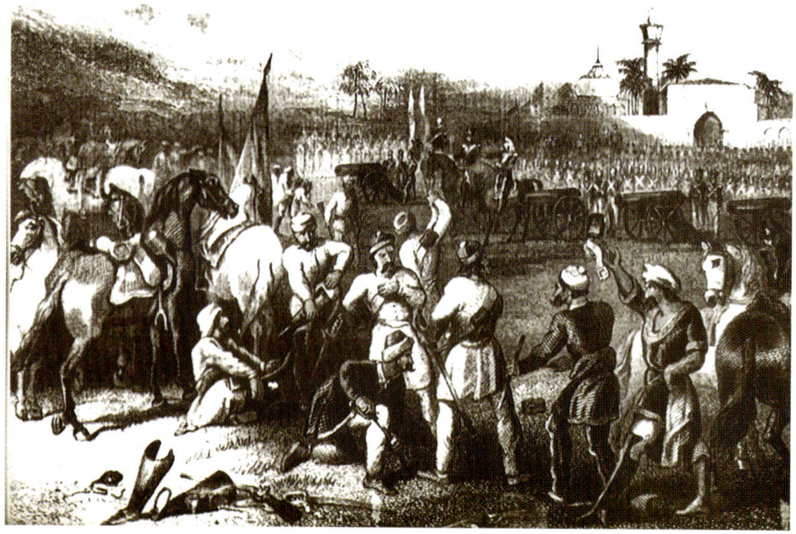

fig. 35. Disarming the Indian soldiers before the war of Independence of 1857, lithoprint.

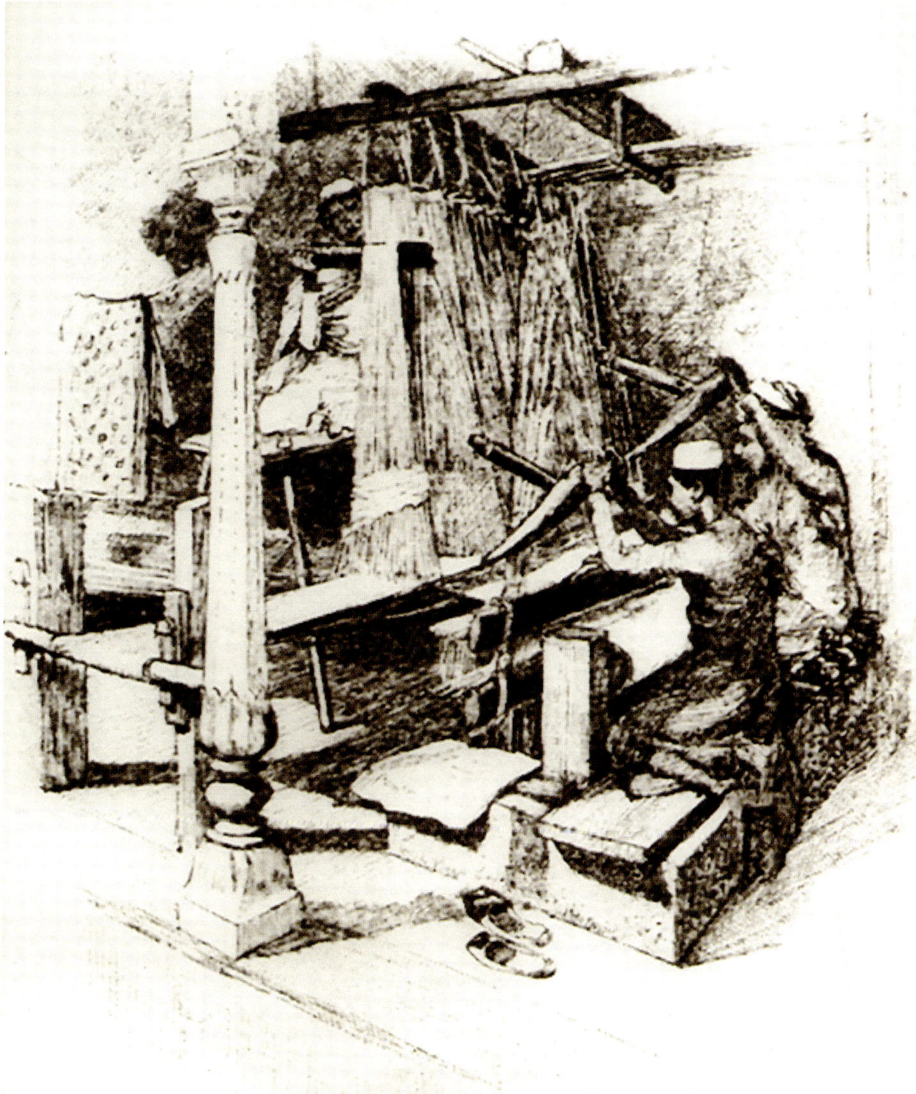

fig. 36. Gold-brocade weaver, paper, linedrawing.

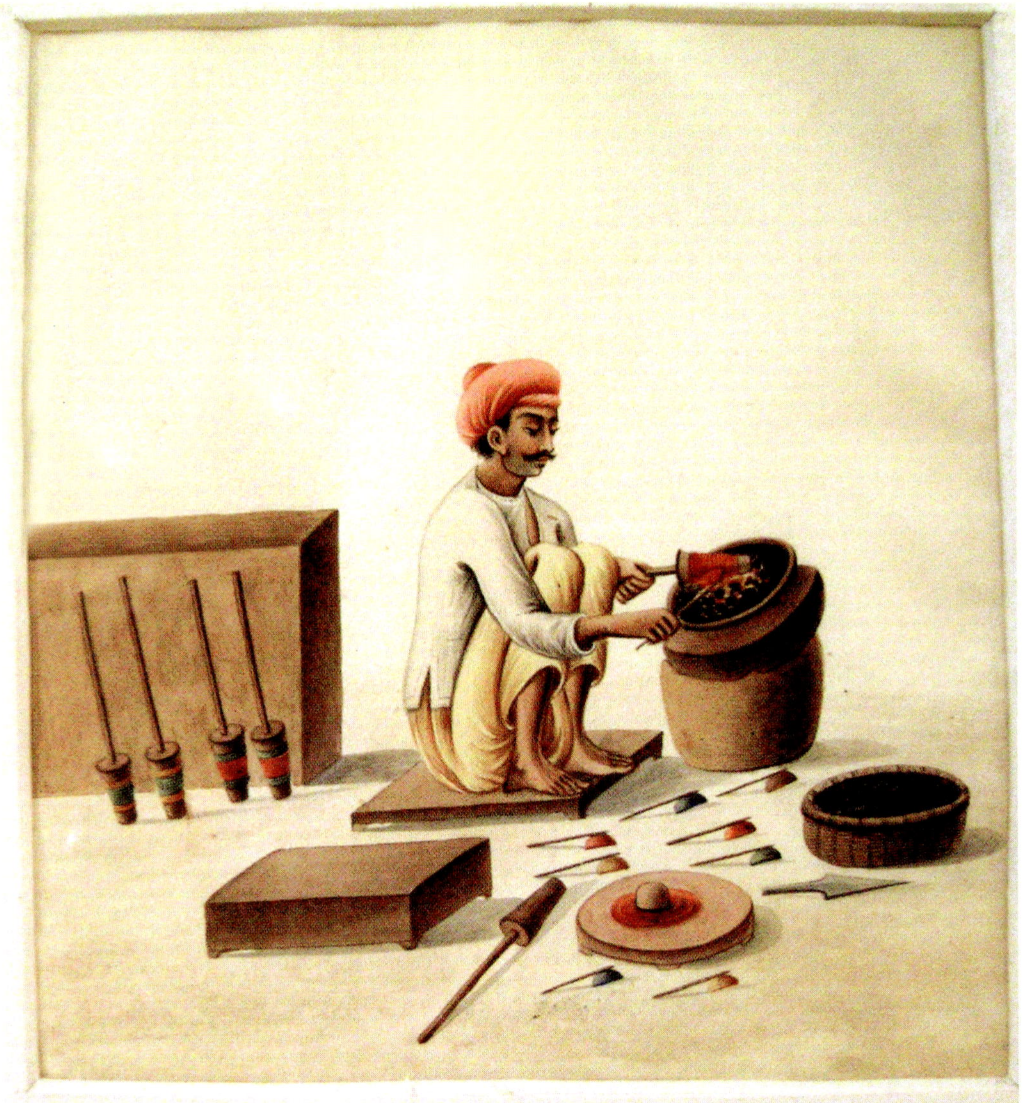

fig. 37.
Bangle maker (*cūḍīhāra*), paper, water colour (Acc. no. 10571).

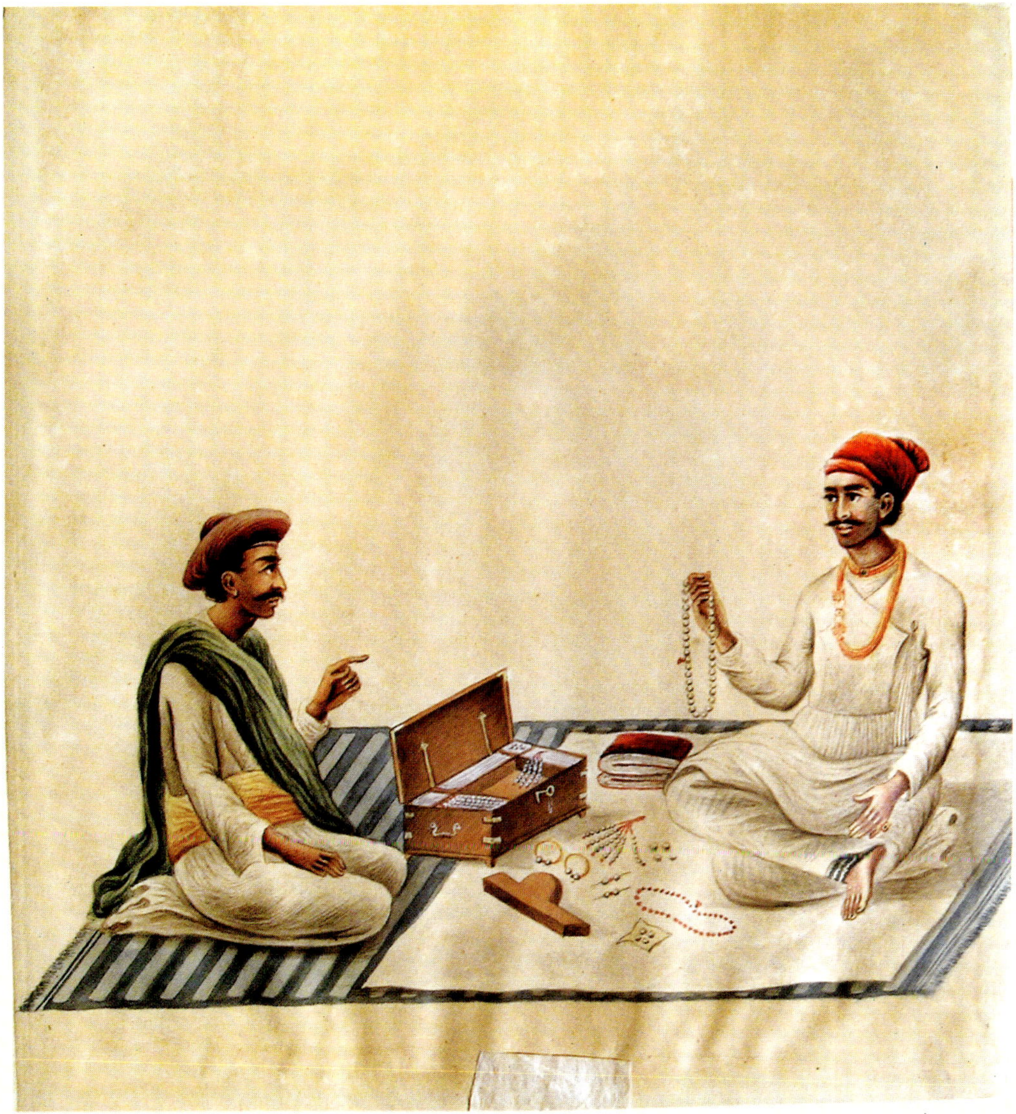

fig. 38.
A Jeweller (*sunāra*),
paper, water colour
(Acc. no. 10570).

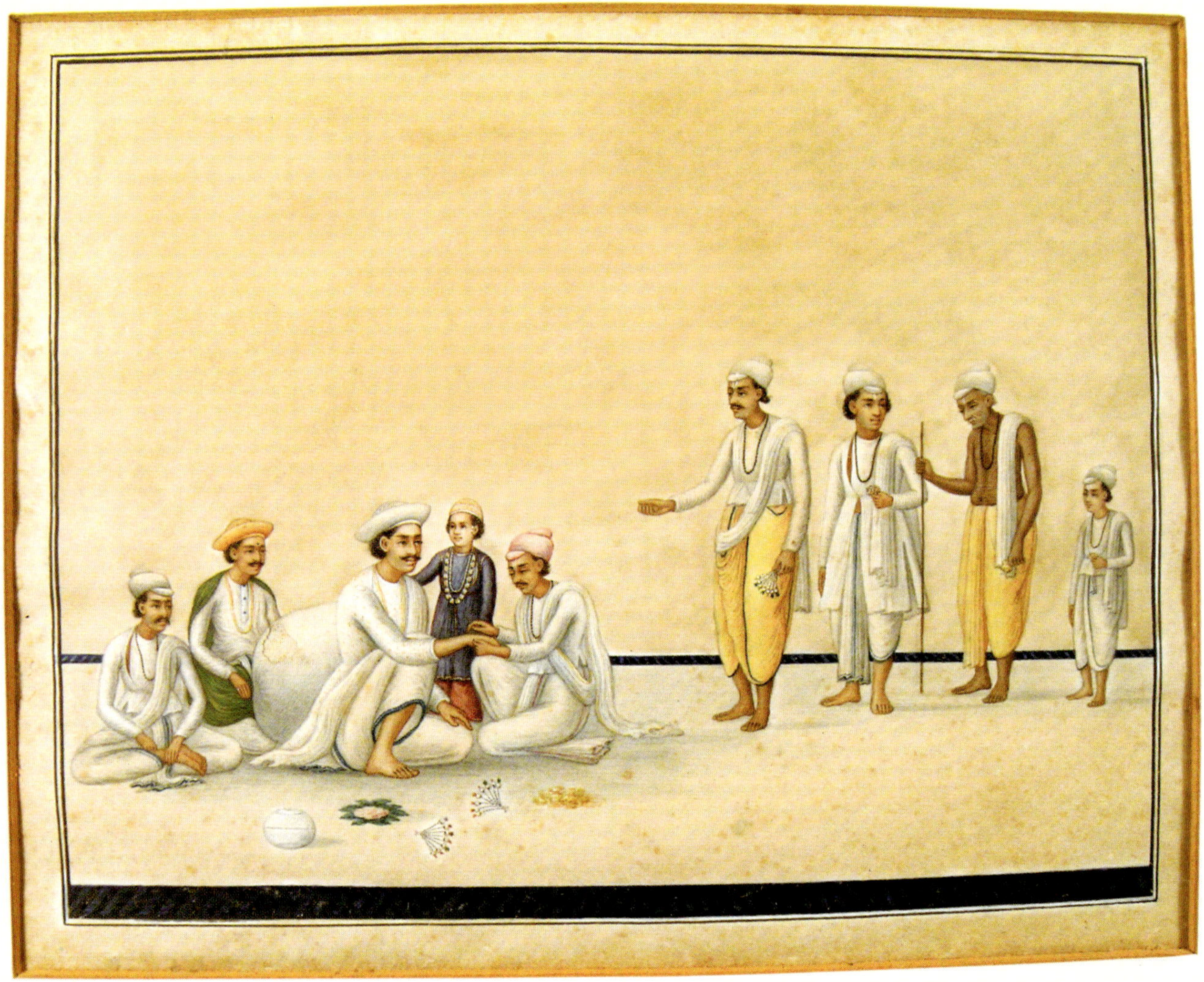

fig. 39. Perhaps *vaidya*, paper, water colour (Acc. no. 1569).

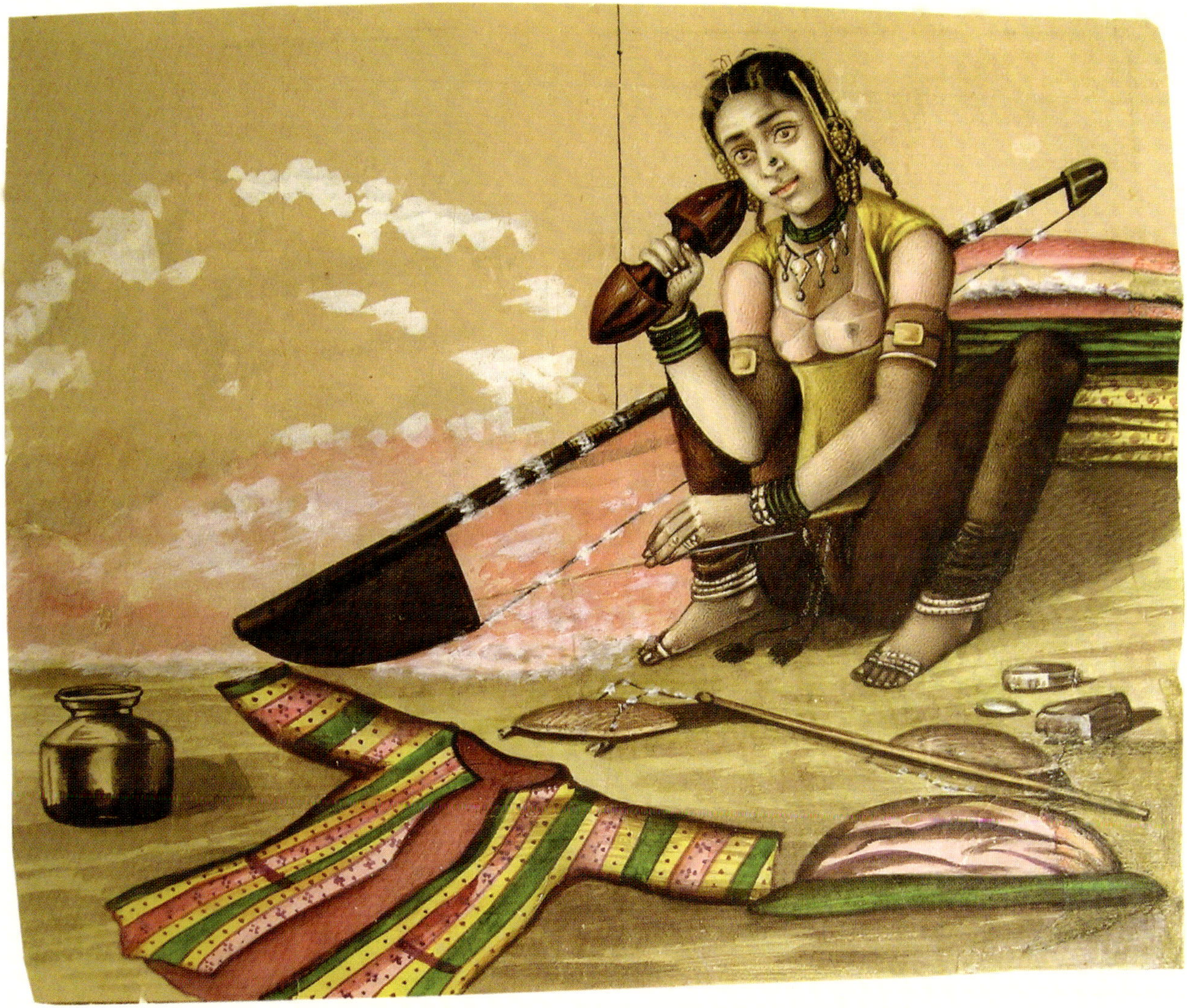

fig. 40. A female *dhuniytāṅ*, paper, water colour (Acc. no. 10818).

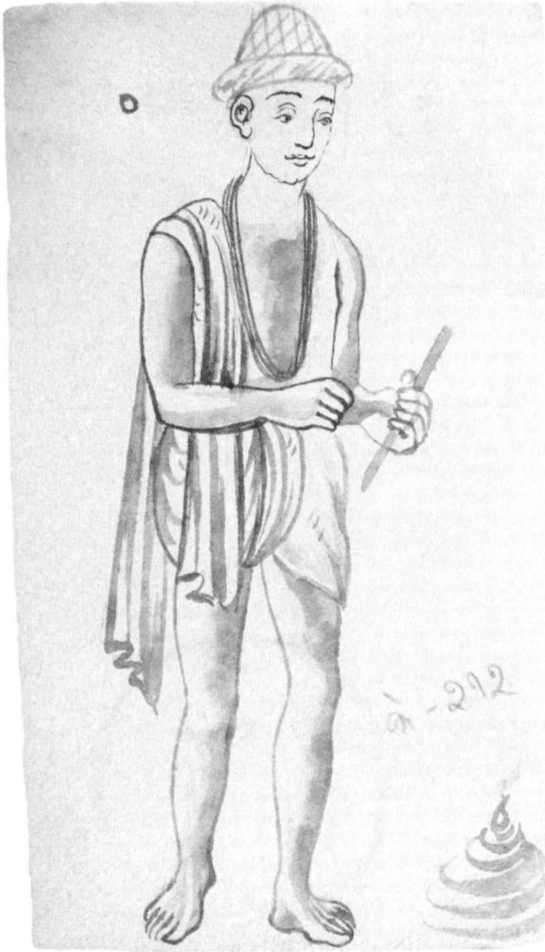

fig. 41. A person knitting thread, paper,
Water colour (Acc. no. 12023).

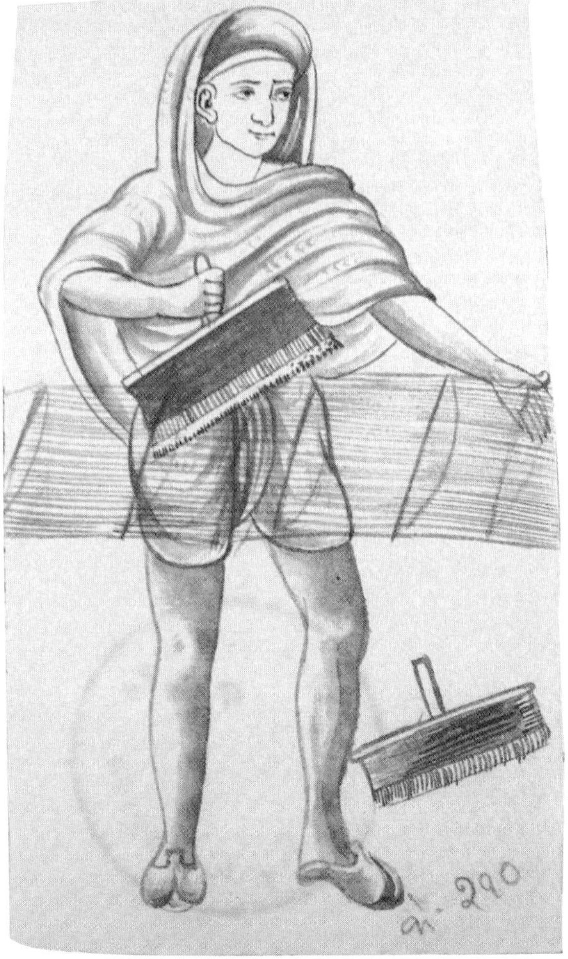

fig. 42. A weaver (*julāhā*), paper,
Line drawing (Acc. no. 12021).

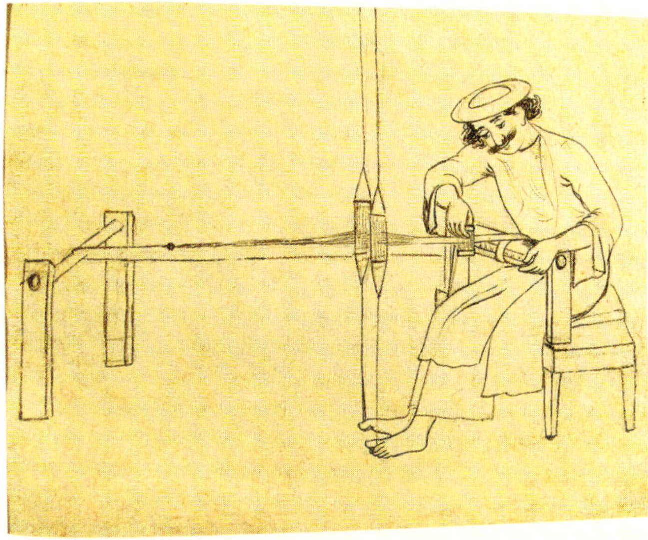

fig. 43. A weaver (*julāhā*),
paper, line drawing(Acc. no. 1573).

fig. 44. A person with fan, paper, water colour.

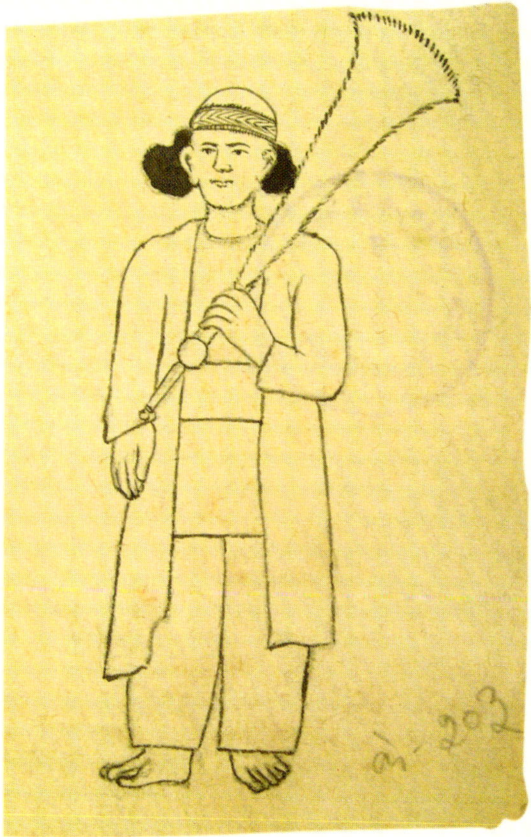

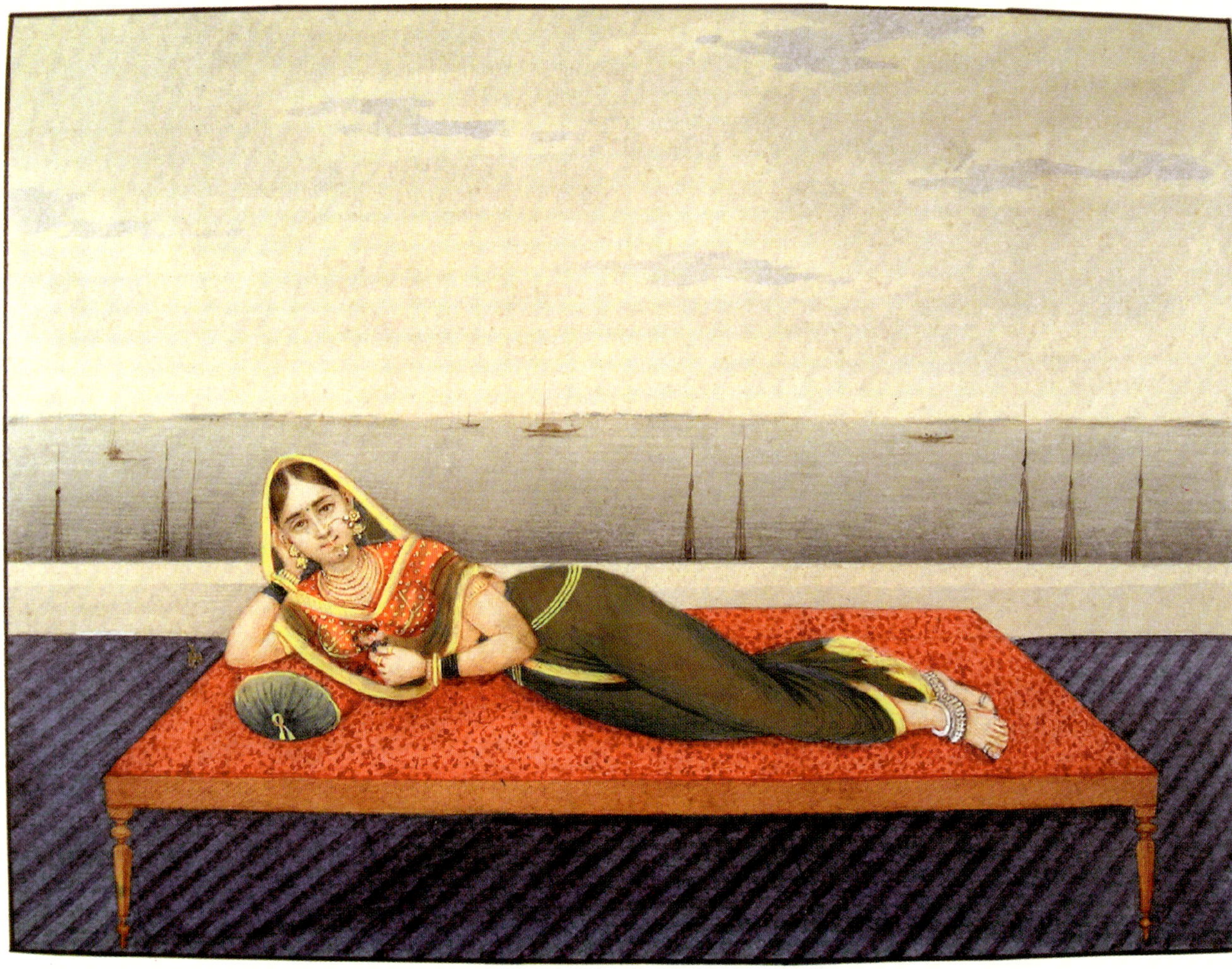

fig. 45. Female on plank, paper, water colour (Acc. no. 1855).

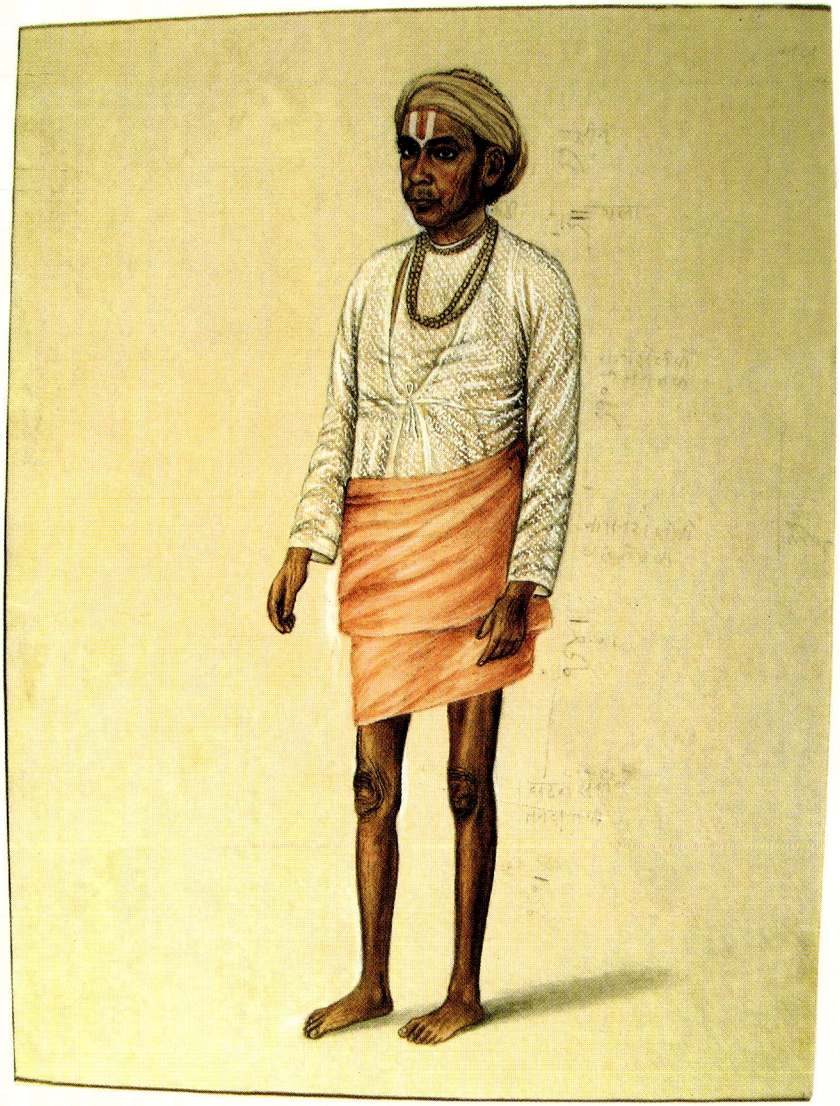

fig. 46. A portrait, paper, water colour (Acc. no. 11527).

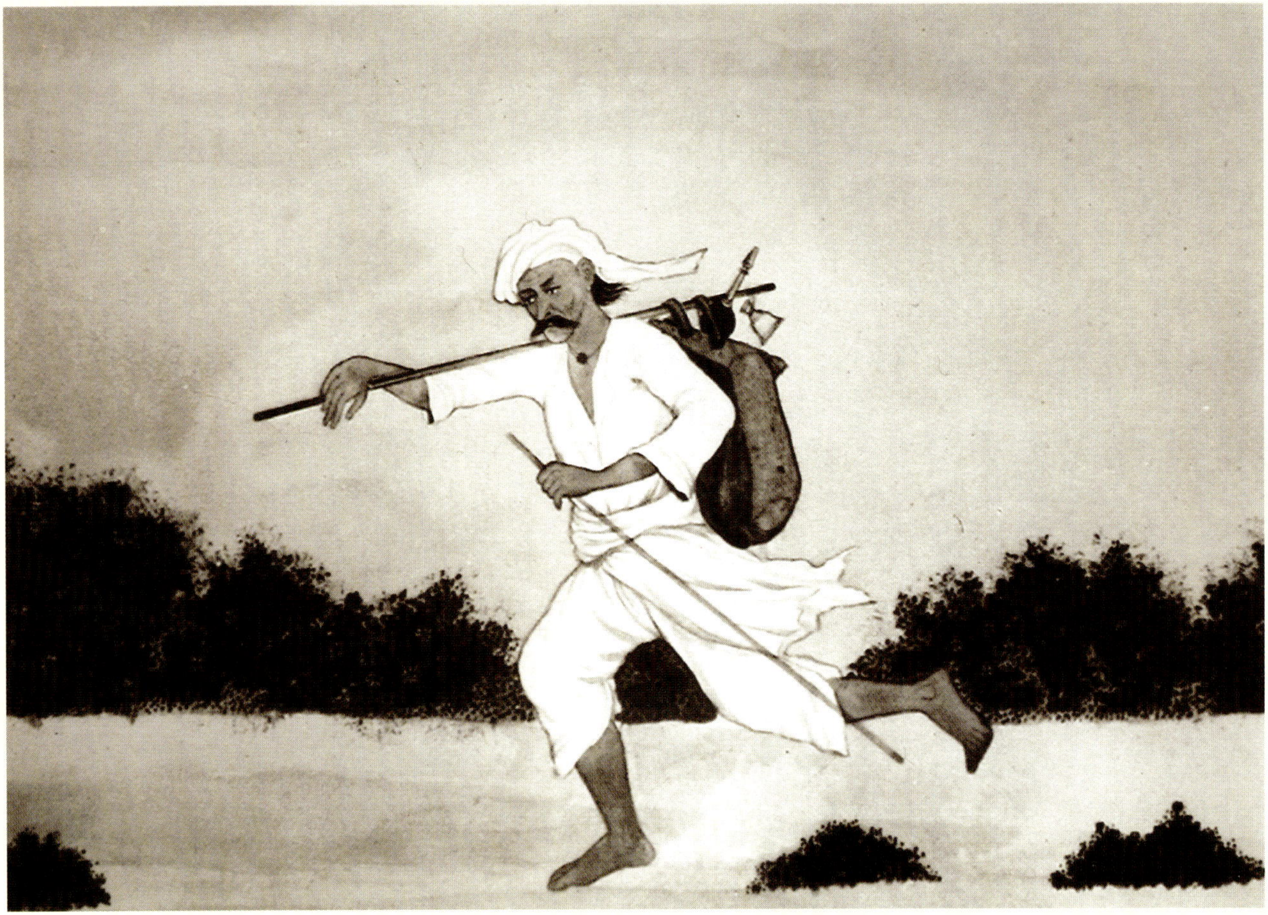

fig.47. Post-runner, paper, line drawing.

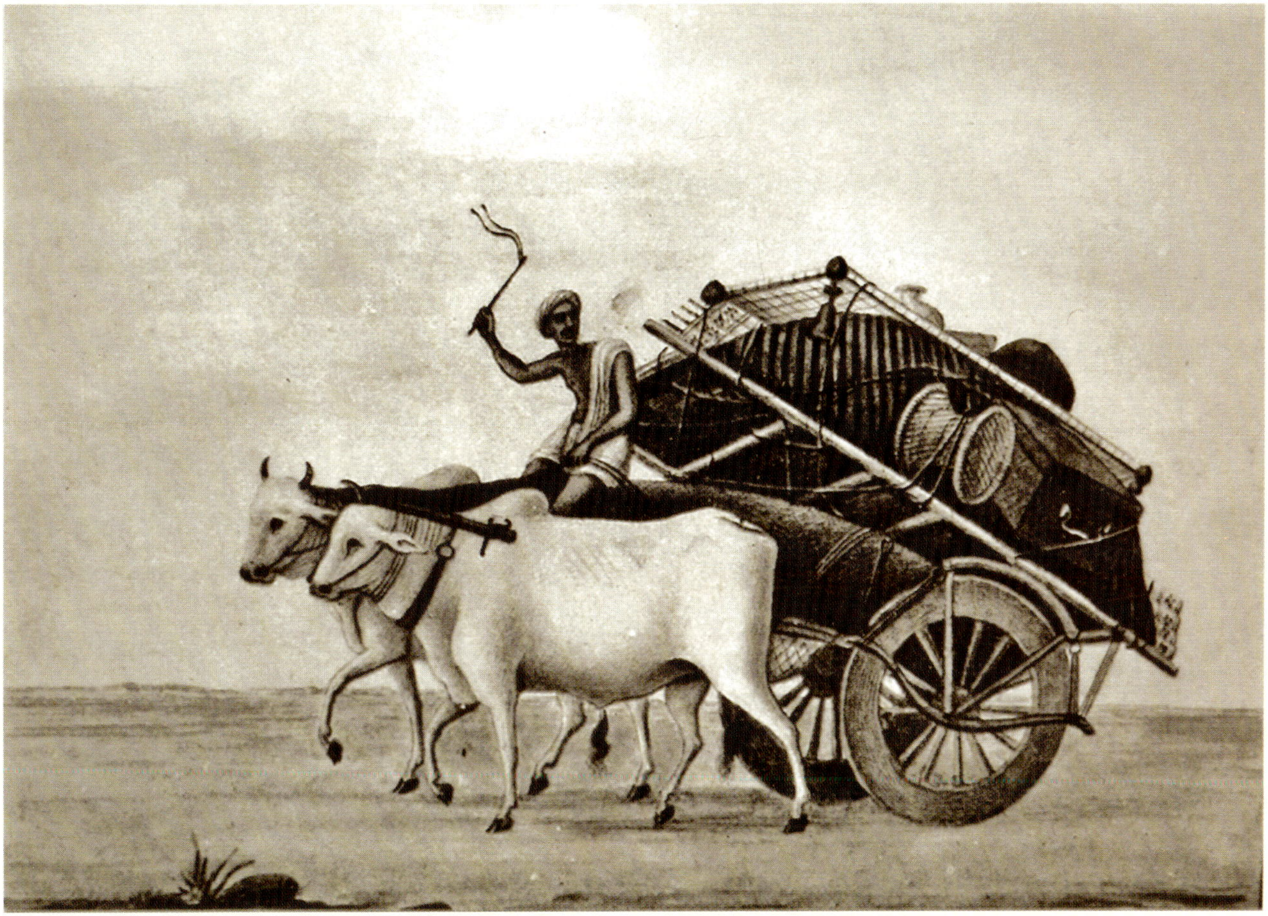

fig. 48. Bullock-cart, paper, water colour.

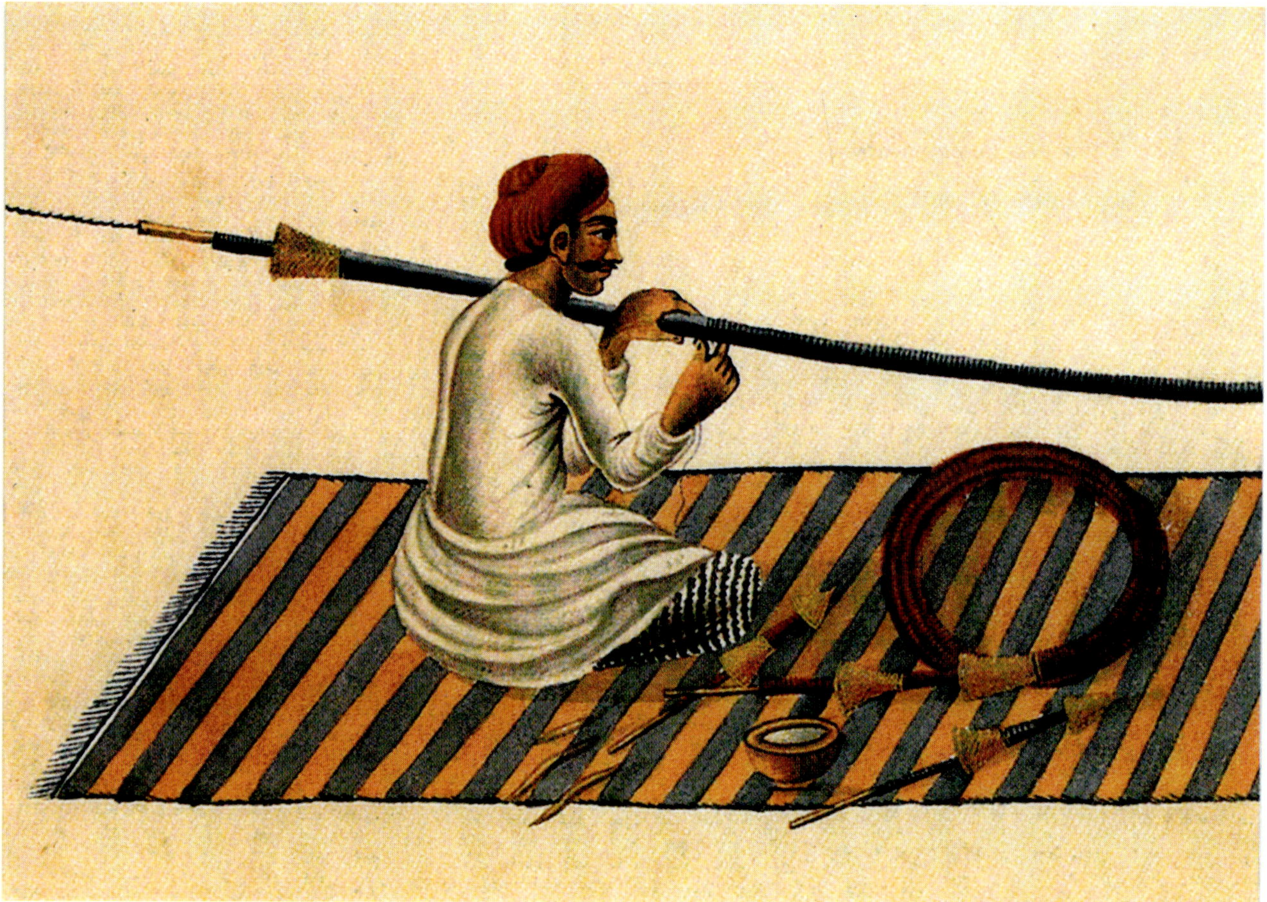

fig. 49. A *Naichbandh* (A *hukkā* steam maker), paper, water colour.

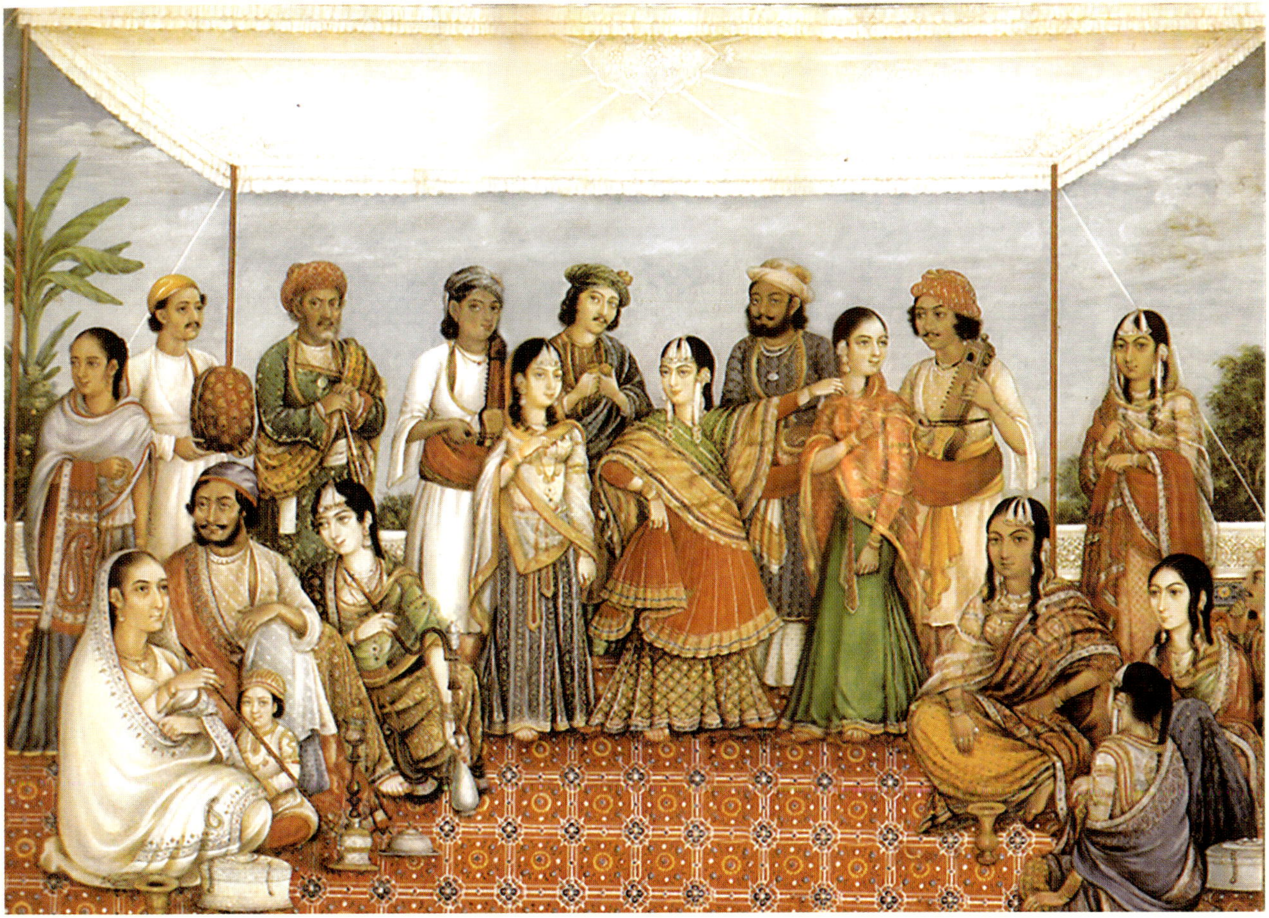

fig. 50. Group of dancing girls and musicians performing beneath a canopy, paper, watercolour.

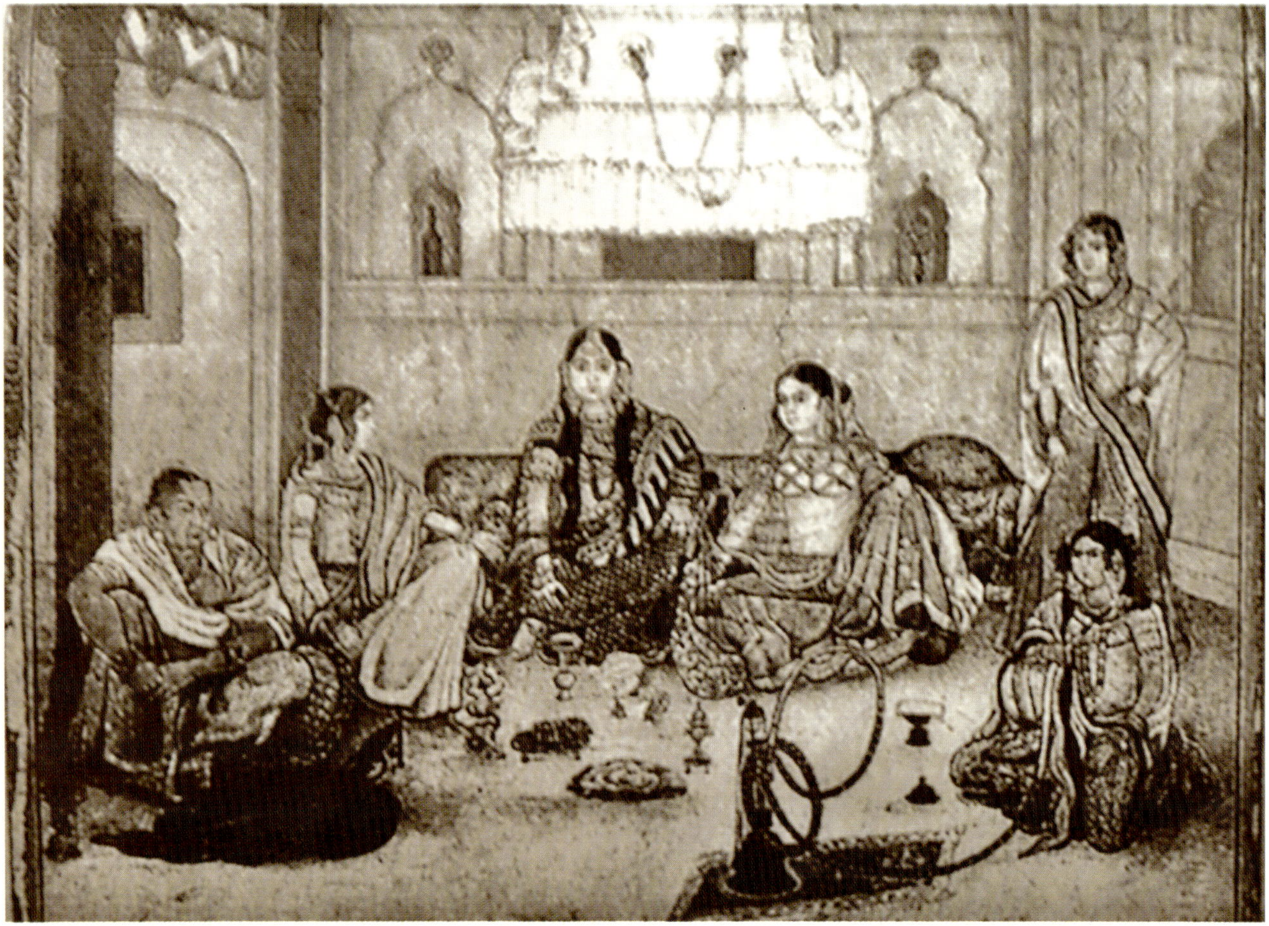

fig. 51. *Janān-khānā*, eighteenth century, paper, water colour.

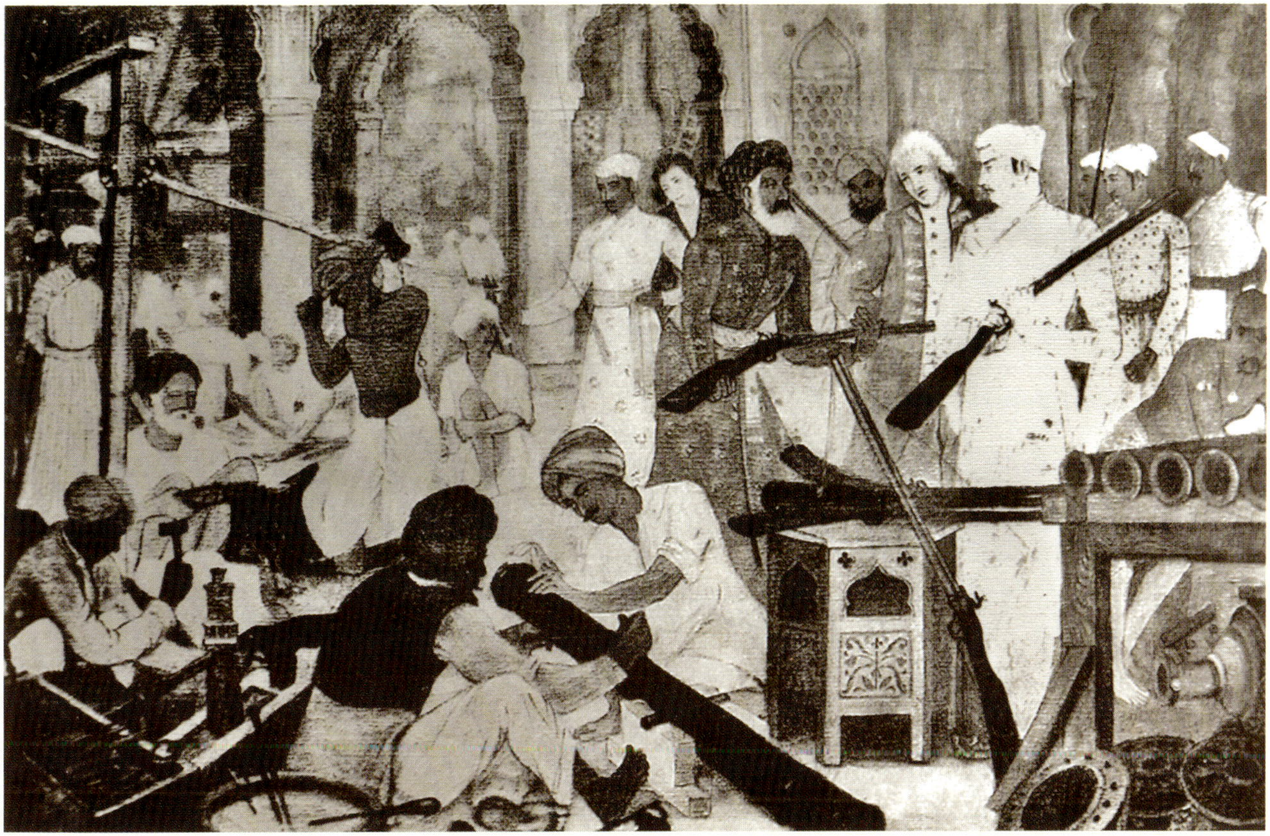

fig. 52. Indian-gun factory, Murshidabad, Bengal, paper, water colour.

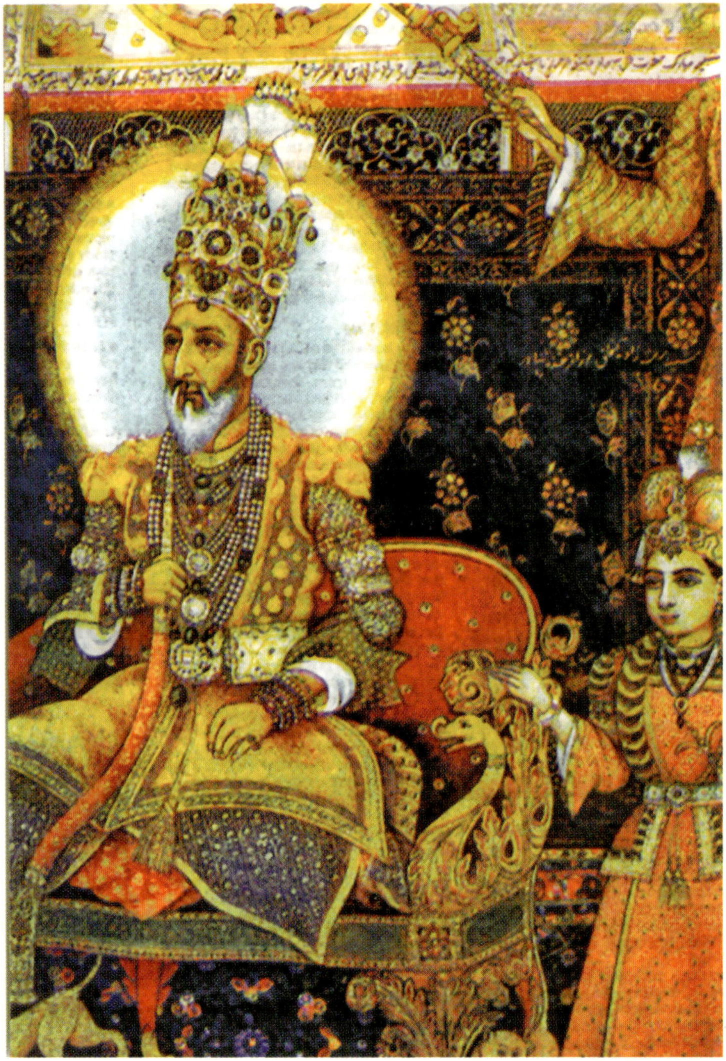

fig. 53. Last Mughal emperor (Bahadur Shah).

Appendix
Artists of the Company School of Art

Agra

1. Latif
2. Gulam Ali Khan
3. Gopal

Amritsar

1. Kapur Singh

Arrah

1. Jagrup Lal

Benares

1. Bihari Lal
2. Chunni Lal
3. Dallu Lal
4. Ganesh Lal
5. Ganesh Prasad
6. Girdhari Lal
7. Kamala Pati Lal
8. Munni Lal
9. Phool Chand
10. Ramanand
11. Shiv Lal
12. Suraj
13. Lal Chand
14. Mahesh Lal
15. Mahesh Prasad
16. Misri Lal

17. Mool Chand
18. Ram Prasad

Bombay

1. Gangaram
2. Joshi
3. James Wales

Calcutta

1. Bhawani Das
2. E.C. Das
3. Manu Lal
4. Sheikh Mohammad Aamir
5. Sheikh Zainul Din

Delhi

1. Faiz Ali Khan
2. Fateh Ali Khan
3. Ghulam Ali Khan
4. Ghulam Murtaza Khan
5. Hasan Khan
6. Ismail Khan
7. Jeevan Ram
8. Khair Mohammed Yusuf
9. Mohammed Ali Khan
10. Mazhar Ali Khan
11. Mirza Shahrukh Beg
12. Mohammed Aalam
13. Mohammed Ibrahim
14. Kumaruddin

Lahore

1. Mohammed Azim
2. Kapur Singh

Lucknow

1. Meher Chand
2. Mammo Jaon

Madras

1. Jaru Naidu
2. Sheikh Abdullah
3. Najibullah
4. Pyare Lal
5. H. Hanumant Rao

Murshidabad

1. Deep Chand

Patna

1. Bahadur Lal
2. Bhawani Das
3. Fakir Chand
4. Gur Sahay Lal
5. Hulas Lal
6. Jai Govind Lal
7. Mahadev Lal
8. Manu Lal
9. Radhe Mohan
10. Sewak Ram
11. Shiv Dayal Lal
12. Shiv Lal
13. Tuni Lal
14. Jai Ram
15. Jamuna Prasad
16. Jamuna Lal
17. Kanhai Lal
18. Ishwari Prasad
19. Bani Lal
20. Jhumak Lal

Poona

1. Damodar Anand Rao Supakar

Puddukkottai

1. Govinda Swami
2. Rama Swami

Tanjore

1. Ravi Naik

Europeans

1. Sir Charles D'Oyly
2. Emily Eden
3. William Daniels
4. Tilly Kettle
5. Capt. Robert Smith
6. James Prinsep
7. Markham Kitto
8. William Hodge
9. Thomas Daniels
10. Alice Grant

11. John Jaipuni or Johann Zoffany
12. Robert Home
13. George Lambert
14. Samuel Scotte
15. Arthur William Davis
16. Ozias Humphry
17. Thomas Hickey
18. Thomas Reives

Bibliography

Agarwal, R.A., *Bhāratīya Citrakalā ka Vikāsa* (Hindi), 1979.

Allan, J. and Dadwell, *The Cambridge Shorter History of India*, Delhi, 1969.

Alvi, M.A. and A. Rahman, *Jahangir the Naturalist*, New Delhi, 1968.

Anand, Mulk Raj, *Album of Indian Painting*, Delhi, 1973.

Appaswami, Jaya, *Indian Paintings on Glass*, New Delhi, 1980.

Archer, F.M., *Indian Miniature in the India Office Library*, London, 1981.

Archer, M. and W.G. Archer, *Indian Paintings for the British*, Oxford, 1955.

Archer, M., *Indian Paintings from Court, Town and Village*, Great Britain; *East India Company*, Apollo, Nov. 1965.

Archer, Mildred, *Patna Painting*, London, 1947; *Company Drawings in the Indian Library*, London, 1972; *Indian Popular Paintings*, London, 1977; *Indian Paintings of the British Period*, London, 1992.

Archer, W.G., *Bazaar Painting of Calcutta*, London, 1953.

———, "Banaras and British Art," *Chhavī*, Golden Jubilee Volume.

Asher, C.B. and Taibote, *India Before Europe*, New York, 2006.

Bale, Charles, *The History of Indian Mutiny*, vols. I & II, London.

Banerjee, A.C. and D.K. Ghose, *A Comprehensive History of India*, vol. IX, New Delhi, 1978.

Basham, A.L., *A Cultural History of India*, London, 1975.

Basu, P., *Oudh and East India Company (1781-1801)*, Lucknow, 1943.

Beach, M.C., *The Grand Mughal Imperial Painting in India 1600-60*, U.S.A., 1978.

Beveridge, A.S. (tr.), *Babur-nama*, rpt., London,

March, 1970.

Bhattacharya, Sabyasachi, *Essay in Modern Indian Economic History*, Delhi, 1987.

Blochman, Abul Fazl (tr.), *Ain-i-Akbari*.

Brown, H., *The Sahibs*, London, 1948.

Chandra, Bipin, Amales Tripathy and Barun De, *Freedom Struggle*, New Delhi, 1972.

Chaudhary, S.B., *Theories on Indian Mutiny*, Delhi, 1965.

Chopra, P.N., B.N. Puri and M.N. Das, *Bhārata kā Sāmājika aura Ārthika Itihāsa* (Hindi), New Delhi, 2001.

Darshan Chitrakar, "Kaśī ke Lok Kalākāra," *Kalā Nidhi*, varṣa 2, aṅka 1, Varanasi.

Rai, Krishna Das, *Bhārata kī Citrakalā* (Hindi), Allahabad, 1974.

Dasgupta, A.C. (ed.), *The Days of John Company*, Calcutta, W.B. Govt., 1959.

Datta, Kali Kinkar, *Survey of Indian Social Life and Economic Conditions in Eighteenth Century (1707-1813)*, Calcutta, 1961.

Dutta, Romesh, *The Economic History of India*, vol. II: In the Vitorian Age 1837-1900, Delhi, 1963.

Farbs, James, *Oriental Memoirs*, London, 1913.

Garder, Brian, *The East India Company*, 1971.

Garola, Vachaspati, *Bhāratīya Citrakalā* (Hindi), Allahabad, 1963.

Giles, Eyre, *Company Paintings India, 19th Century*, London, 1974.

Griffith, Sir P., *The British Impact on India*, London, 1952.

Grover, B.L. and R.R. Sethi, *Studies in Modern Indian History*, New Delhi, 1963.

Gupta, S.P. (ed.), *Readings in Political History of India*, New Delhi, 1976.

Gurmukh, Nihal Singh, *Landmarks in Indian Constitutional and National Development (1600-1919)*, Benares, 1933.

Havell, E.B., "Essays on Indian Art, Industry and Education", *Journal of Indian Art and Industry*.

Hurst, John Fletcher, *Indika: The Country and People of India and Ceylon*, New York, 1891.

Indian History Congress Proceedings, 38th Session, 1977; 41st Session, 1979; 42nd Session, 1981; 45th Session, 1985; 46th Session, 1986; 47th Session, 1987; 48th Session, 1988; Golden Jubilee Session; 53rd Session, 1992-93.

Orwin, John, *Art and the East India Company*, London, 1970.

Jackson, A.V. Williams (ed.), *History of India*, vol. III (in nine volumes), New Delhi, 1987.

Kumar, Dharma (ed.), *The Cambridge Economic*

History of India, vol. 2, *c. 1757 – c. 1970*, Delhi, 1983.

Lalit Kalā, no. 15, 1972.

Majumdar, R.C. (ed.), *The Maratha Supremacy*, Bombay, 1977; *British Paramountcy and Indian Renaissance*, pt. I, Bombay, 1963; *The Mughal Empire*, Bombay, 1974.

Malleson, Colonel G.B., *The Indian Mutiny of 1857*, London, 1891.

Manuk, P.C., "The Patna School of Painting", *Journal of the Bihar Research Society*, vol. XXIV, 1943.

Marg, vol. XLVI, no. 4; vol. VI, 1952-53; vol. XX, 1966-67; vol. XLI, no. 4; vol. XLI, no. 1.

Mehta, N.C., *Studies in Indian Paintings*, Bombay, 1926.

Mehta, Prithvi Singh, *Bihara: Eka Aitihāsika Digdarśana* (in Hindi), Patna, 1940.

Mishra, K.P., *Benaras in the Transition (1738-95)*, New Delhi, 1975.

Mishra, T.N., *Banārasa meṅ Kampanī Śailī kī Citrakalā* (Hindi), Varanasi, 1992.

———, *Westernisation of Indian Art*, New Delhi, 1996.

Moti Chandra, *Technique of Mughal Painting*, Lucknow, 1949; *Kāśi kā Itihāsa*, Varanasi, 1962.

———, "Dakani Kalam; Bījāpur," *Kalā Nidhi*, varṣa 1, aṅka 1, Varanasi.

Mukherjee, Hirendra Nath, *India Struggles for Freedom (A History)*, Bombay, 1948.

Mukherjee, R.K., "Economic History of India (1600–1800)", *The Foundations of Indian Economics*, Allahabad, 1916.

Naqvi, H.K., *Urban Centres and Industries in Upper India 1556-1803*, London, 1968.

Pandey, Banarasi Lal, *Mahārāja Balwant Singh aura Kāśi kā Atīta*, Varanasi, 1975.

Partha, Mitter, *Much Maligned Monsters*, Oxford, Clarendon Press, 1977.

Pillai, P.P., *Economic Condition in India*, 1925.

Puri, B.N., *Special Cultural and Economy History*, 1974.

Rawlison, H.G., *Ancient and Medieval History of India*, Delhi, 2001.

Rupam, no. 5, January, 1921.

Sarkar, Jadunath, *Fall of Mughal Empire*, 4 vols., New Delhi, 1960 & 1966; *History of Bengal*, Delhi, 1973.

Savarkar, Damodar Vinayaka, *1857 kā Svātantrya Samara* (Hindi), New Delhi, 2007.

Seetaramayya, B. Pattabhi, *Economic Conquest of India or The British Empire Ltd.*, Rajamundry, 1937.

Sen, Surendra Nath, *Eighteen Fifty-Seven (1857)*, Delhi, 1957.

Sharma, D.S., *Studies in the Renaissance of Hinduism*, Varanasi, 1944.

Shelvankar, K.S., *The Problem of India* (Penguin).

Smith, Vincent A., *The Oxford History of India*, 3rd edn., London, 1958.

Travels in India:Tavernier, Trans. Bal., 1925.

Travels in Mughal Empire, Bernier, tr. Constable and Smith, 1914.

Verma, Avinash Bahadur, *Bhāratīya Citrakalā kā Itihāsa* (Hindi), Bareilly, 1980.

Vyas, K.C., *The Social Renaissance in India*, Bombay, 1917.

Welsh, S.C. and G.D. Bearce, *Painting in British India (1757-1857)*, Burnwick Maine, 1963.

Welsh, S.C., *The Art of Mughal*, New York, 1963.

William, Dalrymple, *The Last Mughal: The Fall of Dynasty Delhi 1857*, Viking.

Index